Makin' It Right

Makin' It Right

April Joy

iUniverse, Inc.
Bloomington

MAKIN' IT RIGHT

iUniverse books may be ordered through booksellers or by contacting:

iUniverse
1663 Liberty Drive
Bloomington, IN 47403
www.iuniverse.com
1-800-Authors (1-800-288-4677)

ISBN: 978-1-4759-7444-7 (sc)
ISBN: 978-1-4759-7446-1 (hc)
ISBN: 978-1-4759-7445-4 (ebk)

Printed in the United States of America

iUniverse rev. date: 04/26/2013

Introduction

I am now a retired woman who has dealt with many adversities in life and accomplished a successful career in business. Logic tells us that you have to follow a certain path in life to succeed. Well, I followed the illogical path, and I will give people credit—it is not the easiest way to proceed.

I married as a teen, had children, lived in a marriage of domestic abuse, and eventually retired from a successful occupation. Many told me over the years that I should write a book, and finally, I am doing just that. We see much information about girls who marry young and have children. Most of the information is negative, and I do understand why. Some of the basic thought is that they don't understand what they are doing, and I will agree with that today. But if that happens, what can you do? Many say that young mothers or women of domestic abuse will end up having to be subsidized in life by their families, state, or government for the rest of their lives. This may also include their future children. They and their children may have the following hurdles:

- Young women who have children at such a young age may not be able to graduate from high school or earn a college degree.
- Will their children do worse in school than those born to older parents? Are they likely to finish high school?
- Being born to teen moms, will they have behavioral problems, juvenile delinquency, and more conflict with authority?

- Does this mean young mothers will be poor or on welfare because of having a child as a teenager?
- Will their daughters become teenage mothers as well? Will their sons be more likely to end up in prison?
- Will women in abusive relationships be able to get out of it and have a productive life?
- Will the dysfunction in their lives carry on to their children and grandchildren?

Growing up, we often listen to people who give examples to their children of outcomes to the situations I have discussed. Most of the people state all the negative outcomes, and I can understand this. However, from these negative comments come examples of the women who rose above these situations to become successful and fulfilled in life.

I do not want to romanticize the thought that getting married young or having children as an adolescent is a good idea or easy. It is not.

I believe that I accomplished many things and was a prime example of a young mother who strived to make it right despite the odds. Nothing is impossible when we look at the odds and determine to beat them regardless of the norm. I want young girls today to know that success is hard work. It's not easy by any means, but it can be done with determination. We can all do things in our lives that can have a negative impact—it may be drugs, alcohol, or sex—and since we are human, in the end we will have to deal with the outcome.

It is our choice and responsibility to make it right. We may not like it, but we have to take responsibility for our decisions. Some choose not to and may struggle with that decision for the rest of their lives. Others take responsibility and deal with the issues and obstacles that may arise, and believe me it is worth it when you succeed. With perseverance and patience, you can overcome the obstacles and succeed as I have done.

It is my wish that by writing this book, I can inspire young women to understand that even if they have made less-than-perfect decisions, they can turn their lives around and become successful and happy. Additionally, I want women dealing with domestic abuse and violence to know that there is a way out. Hiding what is happening from others is not the answer. There are people out there ready to help you if you want the help and listen.

It may be a long trip, but you can succeed and have a prosperous life with all you could have imagined. It isn't just a dream. Women can have successful careers and take care of their children and themselves in life. Positive outcomes can be yours by accepting responsibility, becoming disciplined, seeking help, and being mindful of those who seek to undermine your goals.

It is my belief that good parents do the best they can with what knowledge they have at the time. Family dysfunction is a fact of life. We need to understand that practicing forgiveness and determining what brought you to the choices you made will bring you strength to make your life what you want it to be. The world is yours to achieve all that your mind can conceive, and your dreams can become reality. I wish you the best.

July 29, 2012

Chapter 1

Makin' It Right

I was the eldest of seven children in a Catholic, middle-class family in Detroit, Michigan. The daily responsibility of caring for my brother and sisters made me grow up fast. I started babysitting around the age of nine and continued until I left home. My mother often turned to me as a surrogate best friend, which was confusing and frustrating for me. A small child cannot possibly fathom the intricate and complicated relationship of her parents, especially when that union is based on constant arguments, violence, alcoholism, and mental-health issues.

There was no time to enjoy a fun-filled childhood. My mother relied on me heavily to take up the slack in the family, which included listening to her frustrations surrounding dealing with my father because of his alcohol use and abuse. While I longed to go outside and play with friends, I felt a huge responsibility to support my mother by cleaning, taking care of my siblings, listening to her fears, dealing with her depressing moods, and doing everything else that goes into caring for a family. Mom did her best to deal with my father by accommodating him and trying to keep peace and make him happy. She became an enabler instead of standing up and insisting on changes for a more peaceful family life for her and her children. I felt robbed of my childhood and longed to become older faster so that I could leave. I dreamed of the day that I would have my own apartment and not have to deal with that kind of life. I longed for a home that would be peaceful and quiet. This seemed like pure freedom.

My first memory of my childhood is of waking up to the police outside as they tried to control my father's drunken rage. I was just three years old. My mother had called the police and was in the yard in the middle of the mess. I was afraid for my mom and did not understand why my dad was being so crazy. The police and my mother were trying to get him to calm down, but he acted like a very angry man who was out of control. This incident was the first experience that led me to be afraid of my dad.

He was a marine in World War II and spent seven years on the island of Iwo Jima, other islands, and Saipan. He went in the service at the age of seventeen, and the war had a dreadful affect on him and eventually on my family.

The amphibious assault on Iwo Jima was considered to be the ultimate storm landing, with a striking force of seventy-four thousand marines. Although planners estimated the attack on Iwo should have been completed within a week or less, they hadn't planned on the stubborn, savvy fighting of the estimated twenty-one thousand Japanese troops on the island.

What started as a quick, violent attack on February 19, 1945, turned into thirty-six days of some of the fiercest and bloodiest fighting the marines had ever encountered. The US Marine Fourth and Fifth Divisions led the invasion with the Third Division in reserve. By the end of World War II, the US Marines, sailors, and soldiers had killed an estimated twenty thousand Japanese and captured more than a thousand prisoners.

The first day saw twenty-four hundred American casualties, and my father was in this battle with one of his best friends. He met John when enlisting, and they became very good friends. Dad was ill prepared to cope with the blood flowing from his fellow soldiers and the violence that made him fear the losses he may have to endure. From listening to Dad, the marines were going on shore in Iwo Jima, and John went with one of the first divisions. John died during the fighting, and I don't believe my dad ever got over that. Dad made few friends but had great allegiance to true friends. Unfortunately, John died, and Dad cried for years over that. His answer to relieving himself of this horrible loss and years of thinking about the other atrocities in that war was to drink more. Of course, the response to drowning his tortured mind in alcohol was devastating to the family.

It became a common occurrence to see my dad being hauled away to jail until he calmed down and sobered up. Dad had some guns in the house. He would scare Mom by taking them out and threatening to shoot her. She had many guns pointed at her in life. The police would take the guns and Dad to jail, but he always found a way to get another one.

The legal system in those days was far more lenient than it is today. The police would come to the house and take Dad to jail, and the next day my mother would go get him and bring him home. Thank heavens things are different today.

For many years Dad was in and out of hospitals, often without his consent, because of his drinking and abusiveness. My mother tried hard to get my dad some help, but he was uncooperative. Dad and Mom were on opposite sides in the courtroom because he wanted out of the hospital. He wanted out, and Mom refused to give in. My dad's mom, however, helped him get out by going to court with him. I think this was about the only thing she did in life that looked like helping him. It actually did the opposite. He did not get the help he needed and came home with us. In the end, Mom lost the battle, and we were back where we started on the roller coaster again.

Dad was a dominating and controlling force in our family, and I feared him all of my childhood. I never understood why my parents argued so much or what it was all about, but I tried to help the best I could. I was definitely afraid when I would wake up in the middle of the night and find my dad drinking. My mother often locked the doors, and Dad would be breaking them down to get in.

My sisters and I were upstairs sleeping, and we were all afraid. I slept in the middle of two of my younger sisters. I felt safer there. Lauren and Susan were just as afraid, and we would cover our heads with our pillows to drown out the noise coming from downstairs. It was crazy. My dad never hurt us; we were afraid because of the screaming, yelling, breaking down doors, and having the police come. I was glad when the police took him away, because I knew it would be quiet for the night and we could sleep.

I loved my dad but wanted him to go away so we could have peace in the family. Mom always talked to me about what had happened. She treated me too much like an adult best friend and criticized my dad to me, which didn't help my feelings toward him. I figured if she was afraid, I should be too. Feeling stuck and frustrated because I had no answers for my mother, I sank myself into taking care of my siblings, doing my chores around the house, and getting away as often as I could to visit with my friends. I was just waiting until I was old enough to get out on my own.

Mom was one of eleven children with three passing away as young children or newborns. I did not know the three who passed away. Of the eight whom I knew, she had three older brothers, two younger brothers, and two younger sisters. Their family was very close and did a lot together.

Grandpa was a carpenter and worked away a lot. At one time, he spent months working offshore, and Grandma was left to run the show. My mom looked up to her own mother and loved her dearly. She would go over and visit as often as she could. Grandma lived about five miles away from us. There were times when I would walk over to her house to visit. I remember having to walk over a bridge to get there and being afraid of the bridge. Today, I look at this little bridge and wonder why I was afraid. We all have fears as children that appear to be big obstacles.

I really don't know if Grandma knew everything that was going on in our home or how serious the situation may have been for our family. I do know she was careful not to get into the middle of things. That was probably wise, because if you knowingly take sides and the couple gets back together, resentment often builds.

Mom had a great relationship with all her brothers and sisters. They thought a lot of her and her of them. We would get together and have great fun visiting and playing with my cousins. Some of life was very normal. We would visit with cousins for holidays, birthdays, and special occasions and enjoy great food, games, fireworks, and our time together as a family. They were moments of pure happiness that I will always remember.

Mom was the oldest of the three girls. Aunt Catherine lived the closest to us, and she was within walking distance of our home. I would go over and visit her, and when I got older, I babysat for my cousins. Aunt Catherine was my godmother and always nice to me. She had six children at that time, and I was very close to all of them.

I went to her house many times, and they helped us out when my dad was being difficult. We often stayed at their home, which, unfortunately, brought havoc to their family. Mom would take all of us to their home after she and Dad had gotten into a battle, and inevitably, Dad would come to their house. He would be yelling and carrying on while my cousins and some of my sisters would hide upstairs in the bedroom. My cousin Theresa still remembers those times and how afraid we all were. Uncle Dan could always seem to calm my dad down enough to get him to go home and sleep it off. He was always looking out for us even though he had a lot of children of his own.

It is tough in a family to bring up your own children and deal with others' issues. I have to give credit to my aunt and uncle for their support. Aunt Catherine and Uncle Dan made a nice home for their children. I would have liked that environment as a kid.

Uncle Dan owned a drugstore across the street from my grandma's house. I would go over and help at the drugstore.

It got busy when the Chevy plant employees ended their workday. I remember spending many days standing on the corner collecting contributions for poppies sold by the Blue Star Mothers for the veterans. These are all good memories.

Aunt Rosemary was sixteen when I was born and was the youngest girl. I thought she was the greatest growing up because we did a lot together when I was young. She spoiled me as a youngster, and I was the first grandchild who lived close to home. I was the flower girl in her wedding and was very upset when she got married. Extended family can be so important in our lives.

My mom's brothers were all very different in the family. Uncle Darrell was the oldest; he was very tall and happy-go-lucky. He lived on a farm after the war, and I remember going to his house to visit. One of the main reasons I remember the farm is because of all the animals. I was not used to animals, and being from the city, this was a very different environment. My cousin Kathy was their only daughter, and she was a few months older than me. We were not close only because we did not see each other often.

Uncle Jeff worked for the phone company and was such a nice guy. When I moved away, he would hook me up with my mother to talk on the phone. At that time, it was very expensive to make long-distance calls. He unexpectedly passed away in his forties from a heart attack, and this was a shock for the family. He was truly missed, and his wife and children were devastated by his death. He was very close to all of the family—such a great man.

I didn't know Uncle Ernie very well, and eventually they moved from Michigan to New Mexico. He rarely visited any of the family after moving away.

I was the flower girl for Uncle Ned's wedding. He later divorced, and my two cousins ended up living with my grandparents for many years. Two of my mom's brothers were in World War II, and happily, they both came home safely. My mother's youngest brother, Uncle Larry, married when I was about twelve years old, and we moved away after this.

My grandparents were quite unique. I truly loved both of them, especially my grandma. I spent a lot of time with her, and she was a tough lady. She was a true Irish lady, a staunch Catholic, and a Blue Star Mother. She was very involved with the veterans and spent lots of time making potato salad and baked beans for them. She had me peel potatoes and help with the cooking as a child. I loved every bit of the time that I spent with my grandma.

I was one of the oldest of about thirty grandchildren, and most of my cousins remember Grandma as someone they were afraid of. To me, she was just a stern lady, and no one messed with her. I respected that as a child and understood it. I also knew where she hid all the candy.

My mother was very close to her mom and spent a lot of time at her house. She had a hard time when we moved away, because she missed her family so much. My dad was not very sympathetic, and I think he resented the relationship Mom had with her family. This created conflict between them as well.

Because of the big differences in Mom's and Dad's families, I do believe that she was ill prepared to deal with Dad's problems after the war. Today we call it post-traumatic stress disorder, but it wasn't even recognized then.

Before Dad returned from the war, the marines sent him to a place in Washington that helped soldiers returning to their families. Dad was impatient to get home. He thought he was fine and wanted to come home, so he did. It was only reasonable that Mom thought he would be fine, and upon his return, they set their wedding date. Times were very different then. Emotional issues were thrown under the rug, and people were often in denial.

Much later, I grew to understand my father better and realized that the war affected him forever. The events of the war plagued his mind and soul until the day he died of lung cancer in 1997. Dad lacked a supportive and loving family life when he was growing up, which also explains a lot. His parents broke up when he was only five years old, leaving him to fend for himself at that tender age when children need guidance and security in order to grow into stable adults.

My father had one brother, Uncle Jake. He was my godfather and had six children of his own. Uncle Jake joined the army, and when the war came about, he went to Canada. He met his wife and got married there. My dad went to war. I am sure this created a conflict between the two of them. Their standards of supporting the United States were much different.

As a child, I saw Uncle Jake as friendly, funny, and great to be around. Grandma Gladys always favored him and his children, but I never knew why. Unfortunately, Dad was on the outside looking in. It is too bad when we make one child feel less or not as important as another.

When Dad and Uncle Jake were children, Grandma Gladys worked different shifts, which left them both to their own devices to wander the streets of downtown Detroit. Eventually, she divorced my grandfather and pitted the children against him. My dad took her side and supported her, while Uncle Jake continued to see his dad and take his side.

Grandma Gladys worked as a seamstress and later in life at a bar that a friend of hers owned. From what I understand, she worked in the speakeasies during the time of prohibition. She was a feisty lady and drank quite a bit of alcohol herself. Dad rarely saw his own father after their divorce and did not want any of his children to be around him. My brother Ted is the only one who ever met him. With the dysfunction Dad lived through during his childhood, it is no wonder he was ill prepared to raise a family of his own.

Dysfunction is generational in that we learn how to act from how our parents act and how we are treated and respected while growing up. If we feel little love and are not valued, we learn to disrespect others, and our ability to perceive and give love is thwarted. We become filled with shame and guilt even though the family dynamics were not our fault. We learn to draw deep into ourselves through fantasies and dreams that help us cope with the misery around us. It is not until we reach adulthood and escape into the real world on our own that we begin to understand the why and how of it all. And some of us do not ever understand.

Most people who live in families with difficulties try to make the best of it—at least in my family they did. We try to do things for our children that appear to be normal. We encourage them to succeed and try to give them as much as we can. We are not always aware of the negative impact that may be evolving in our lives.

My parents were financially successful for quite a few years when I was young. I took dance lessons from about the age of four until I was about thirteen. Dad was always excited about recitals and took pictures all the time. He was very upset with me at my first recital, because I was afraid to go out on the stage. They tried everything to get me to go out, but I refused. A lot of my family attended, and Dad had a fit because I would not come out on the stage. On the way home, he gave me a devil of a time. I was only four years old and learned that I had better go out on the stage the next time or else.

My mother made all my costumes for all my recitals each year. She was a great seamstress. She often made costumes for the other girls in my class also. This part of my life is a happy memory. Mom always encouraged us to dance and have a good time. My grandma Mildred, who was my mother's mom, was very supportive and took me and other children with her to dance for the veterans on several occasions. She was very involved in her church, and as part of the Blue Star Mothers, she put on a show for the veterans every year until she got very sick. After World War II, many women got involved helping the veterans coming home from the war. This was especially true in the case of my grandma; she had her sons come home safely, and she felt very fortunate for that. Maybe that is why she did so much to help the veterans.

My grandma Mildred was my grandfather's second wife. Grandpa's first wife died shortly after giving birth to their daughter, Ruth. From what I understand, Grandpa was very distraught after his wife's death and had a little girl to take care of. He soon met my grandmother, and they married. Ruth became part of the family and was quite a bit older than the rest of the eleven children. My grandmother took care of Ruth and her own eleven children, so I guess that made it an even dozen. Ruth passed away before I was born. Ironically, she died having her first child.

To me, Grandpa was a quiet man who chewed tobacco and was always remodeling the house. As each child left home, he would take over his or her room and make a small apartment. My grandparents had a huge home, but by the time everyone had left, Grandma was living in three rooms and sharing a bathroom with a tenant. He was always looking for ways to make money, even renting parking spaces in the driveway to guys who worked at the factory.

Grandma Mildred was the dominant figure in the household. She made a family for her children, which was much different from my dad's family. My mom's family did a lot together. Grandma organized family reunions at the park each year and made sure we were all there. Someone would have a Christmas party, and we would all get together. The parties were always big, because we had a big family. Every once in a while, my uncles would drink a bit too much and get into a brawl. They would make up later, and life would go on. Once Grandma passed away, the traditions dwindled.

As a child, it was my greatest desire and prayer to escape the negative parts of the world that I lived in with my brother and sisters into a wonderful life with my own family. Little did I know that I would be leaving home much sooner than I had thought.

Because I was the oldest, my job was more about babysitting or taking care of my brother and sisters. I helped by babysitting, cleaning house, and being a friend to my mom. My dad accused her of being a friend to me instead of a mother. In hindsight, he was right, but at that time, I was on my mom's side. If my dad came home drunk and she could not handle the situation, she would wake me up and have me get my dad to go to bed. Normally, by that time he was upset and crying over his past, looking for answers that never came. That made me feel bad for him; I knew he would go to sleep, and the unsettledness would end for us kids for that night. I always knew that there would just be a small window of time before it would happen all over again.

I grew up too fast and looked out for my brother and sisters. A lot of the time I felt they were a pain in the neck because I would have to take one of my sisters with me to visit friends. My brother Ted was only a year younger than me, and he was the only one whom I didn't have to worry about taking care of. As a boy, he had different responsibilities in the family. At that time, boys took out the garbage and worked in the yard. They didn't have to worry about cleaning the house or doing the dishes. That was work for the girls. My dad was hard on him, and at times, I was glad that I didn't have to help Dad with the projects that Ted helped him with. If Ted made a mistake, Dad yelled at him, and Ted had to deal with the criticism.

I started babysitting for others at twelve and did a good job taking care of kids. I had learned at a young age how to watch out for the kids. I have to admit that at about the age of thirteen, I had a boy named Michael come over to visit me while babysitting. He was sixteen and in the public high school. I had a crush on him, and we used to meet at the park. My mom happened to come over to the house where I was babysitting and caught Michael at the house. She had a fit and laid down the rules. She checked on me often after that to make sure I was alone. I was always trying to find a way to do what I wanted.

At a very young age, I would spend time with my friends and go out to spend time with boys. I remember going to a friend's house and sneaking out in the middle of the night. We hitchhiked into town, met some guys, and drove around. They then dropped us off at home. I thank God today that I was a lucky girl and wasn't picked up by some crazy people and hurt. We do so many things when we are young that are dangerous, and we don't even realize it.

When my sister Marie was born, I spent a lot of time taking care of her. Aunt Rosemary was concerned about how much time I spent taking care of kids and helping out and had invited me to go to her home for the summer. I was about twelve years old. My aunt had a baby while I was there and left me to take care of her daughter while she was in the hospital.

My uncle came into my room one night and tried to show me what life was about. I threw him onto the floor and told him to leave me alone. I did not tell my aunt but did tell my mother what he had done. I was afraid my aunt would turn against me, so I didn't tell her. I always felt bad that I didn't tell her, and when I got older, she asked me if my uncle had ever bothered me. I still couldn't admit it, and I feel bad about it today. I felt guilty about it happening and did not want to deal with it even as an adult.

He tried this with many other cousins, and she found out what he was like eventually. Many years had gone by before she found out who he truly was as a person. By this time, she had six grown children. She passed away many years later, and I miss her to this day. My mother never told my dad, because she felt he would go nuts and cause upheaval.

When I came home from my aunt's house, I felt my sister Marie didn't know me. She was only about ten months old at that time. After that, I didn't take care of her as much and spent more time with friends.

My dad was a very smart man, and without any college, he started a business fixing televisions and installing antennas on houses. Technically, he was brilliant and patented a few things during his lifetime. In spite of the drinking and arguments, Dad held great aspirations for his girls and instilled in us a belief in ourselves that we could do anything we put our minds to.

Once I began my career, I never felt that it was a man's world like so many others believed. I thank Dad for teaching me to be determined and succeed. In spite of all of the dysfunction, that was one thing Dad was able to get through to me.

Dad soon excelled in his business and built a larger building that provided more room for selling televisions and a repair business. He went into business with another friend who did the selling while Dad did the repair work.

I was about five years old when Dad built a new house for us where we lived very comfortably. I went to work with him on Saturdays and watched everything he did. When I got older, I had no problem removing the back from a television and pulling out all the tubes to fix a problem. I would go to the drugstore and use a tube tester to find out which one needed to be replaced. Dad would always tell me, "Just stay away from the high voltage when you are in the back of that set." This catalyst was to lead me into a satisfying career later on in life.

Mom helped Dad with his business, and we had many good years. They had their battles, but things went on as normal. The house was nice, and we were very fortunate to have a lot in our lives at this time. When I was about eleven years old, my dad was spending a lot of time at the bars. My mother decided to go to the bars with Dad. Since she couldn't change him, she thought joining him at the bars might be a solution. Calling around to find them and see when they would be home was the norm. Once they did return home, the situation would either be peaceful, or Mom would call the police to have Dad taken to jail because he got out of hand. The next day's soberness brought her to a decision to drop charges and have him released. Such was life.

Mom did not realize that she had become Dad's enabler. Few had heard of the concept of enabling in those days. She enabled him by going to the bars with him or rescuing him from jail instead of letting him sit there and think about what he had done. Life always gives us consequences for our choices whether good or bad. When people, no matter what age they are, consistently get out of consequences for bad behavior, they never have the opportunity to learn to do better. They also aren't motivated to do so. Why should Dad decide to stop drinking and gain control of his life? Mom was always there to bail him out and bring him home as if nothing happened, only to have it start all over again. By always rescuing him, he never had a reason to straighten up.

One evening, Dad got very drunk and tore the phone off the wall. Dad tended to throw things when he got mad. He would have a drink in his hand and heave it across the room. My mom would be on the telephone calling the police while all hell was breaking loose.

I can honestly say my mom did antagonize him at times. I remember listening to her yelling, and I would think, *Mom, please shut up.* Oftentimes, things would not have gotten out of control if she could have kept quiet. As a child, this was what I thought, but as an adult, I know it would have just happened at another time. Mom finally decided to leave Dad and had found a place for some of us to stay. She took my youngest sister Marie and I with her.

The priest at church got involved trying to help us out. We had to go by our home for some reason—I don't remember why—and the car we were riding in broke down in front of the house. I remember being so afraid that we would not get out of there before my dad woke up and found us outside. I saw that he had thrown a coffee table through the front picture window and could only imagine what else he had done. Needless to say, he didn't wake up, and we left. Within a couple of weeks, Dad convinced Mom to come home.

Dad lost his business and had to take a job in Pontiac commuting home on weekends. The drive to Pontiac was a couple of hours from our home, so he stayed in an apartment during the week and came home on weekends. He missed us and hated the traveling. One night while driving home late, he fell asleep at the wheel and got into a serious accident. He was in the hospital for quite some time with serious injuries. I hate to say it, but life was much quieter for a while.

Dad appreciated having ultimate authority. His main way of discipline was to pull down our pants and spank us when we were little. It was embarrassing, and I hated it. His second method was to take away an item that meant a lot to us, and we would never see it again. Once he made me give up a beautiful necklace of mine for acting up in church. Mom thought I would have minded the rules, but his discipline of choice just caused me to think of ways to do what I wanted and not get caught. I learned to become a good liar and was convincing. That was not a good decision, but children seek ways to just be able to survive in a house full of craziness.

As time went on, Dad had to find a job to keep the family together, and we were losing our home because of foreclosure. After much searching, the only position he could find was in North Dakota. That was a long way away, and none of us were happy about that. In the back of my mind, I always thought it would never happen. All our family and friends were where we lived, and I could not believe we were moving. I also had a crush on my friend Michael and did not want to leave him.

Dad accepted the job and left for North Dakota, taking my brother Ted with him. He knew that if he took Ted, my mother and the rest of us would follow, and we did. We left our home and took what we had left to North Dakota. I cried all the way because I'd had to leave Michael. What do we know when we are kids?

Chapter 2

Life in North Dakota

In 1960, when I was thirteen years old, we moved to North Dakota. Life was quieter with fewer arguments, and Dad really liked his job. I think he was beginning to settle down a bit. Maybe part of it was that he was maturing and getting older. There was much less craziness than when we lived in Michigan. I cried on the plane all the way to North Dakota because of leaving Michael.

We landed on a small runway in North Dakota, which was very different than Detroit. Being from a big city, it was very different from what I was used to. Grand Forks had one movie theatre and not a whole lot more. Oh my, what a difference.

North Dakota is significantly different than Michigan. It was a much more rural environment with smaller cities. The TV station went off the air at eleven o'clock after the news. On the weekends, it might have been twelve thirty. Oh boy—quite an adjustment. I started school in ninth grade and was very uncomfortable. I had gone to the same school with my friends for eight years, and this was like starting over again. I knew no one, and the environment was totally different. My school in Michigan was a Catholic school and very strict. Mom and Dad could not get me into the only Catholic school in the city, so it was off to the public school.

At that time, there was a big difference in the curriculum and the rules. For me, the public school was pure freedom. I didn't know anyone and made some friends, but it wasn't the same as in Michigan. The school sponsored dances in downtown Grand Forks for the high school students and allowed the soldiers at the army base to attend. Bad idea—most of the soldiers were too old to be dating high school girls. Of course, I didn't think it was a bad idea at the time. Most teenage girls wouldn't.

I was devastated by having to leave my so-called boyfriend, Michael, my friends, my cousins, and especially my grandma. I had four younger sisters and one brother when we moved to North Dakota. My relationship with my brother and sisters at that time was based on being their caretaker, and I had not developed close relationships with them.

My sister Susan was around nine years old when we moved, and she helped out a lot with the rest of the kids. She was the only sister who helped clean and take care of things. She was very young at the time, and little did I know, she would take over my responsibilities after I left home. I looked at the others as just kids, except for my brother who was a year younger.

Ted had his own issues with my dad, and the two of us were so close in age that it was more of a competition. My dad always gave him a hard time about his grades at school. I would get As, and he got Cs. After I left home, he got As. Go figure. I was a very difficult older sister and gave him a hard time. Ted was a good brother and very quiet. He knew about many things I did that would have upset my parents, but he never told them. I was probably competing more with him than he was with me. Let's just say that I was a bossy sister who liked being the oldest.

I was fourteen years old when I met Dean in March 1962 in North Dakota. He was seventeen, and we met through a mutual friend who I worked for as a babysitter. Dean had come to visit his friend, and we met there. He was stationed at the army base in Grand Forks, North Dakota. I told him my age the first night we met, and he decided not to see me again. Friends and I would hang around the USO in town, and I saw him there. Young high school girls were not allowed to go into the USO because of their age, so we stayed outside. One night my friend Melba wanted to go to the drive-in, so we asked Dean if he wanted to go with us. We all piled in the car and had a fun time. Dean and I started seeing each other after that night. I guess he changed his mind about my age.

My first impression of Dean was that he was a nice guy, fun to be with, and very good-looking. He was very attentive and seemed like a great person to be with so we became involved quickly. From the standpoint of a fourteen-year-old, I had met the man of my dreams; I was so excited to have such a fine-looking boyfriend. It was a magical time in my life, and I had someone who truly cared about me. After all, what I saw on the outside was surely proof of what kind of person he was on the inside. That outward appearance can often be otherwise, but at my age, looks can be deceiving. If I could give any advice to young girls today, it would be to never take another person at face value. People are complicated and rarely show their true selves until you get to know them well, which can takes years.

I began lying to my parents about Dean. They would not have approved of me having a boyfriend at that time in my life. Dad would have a fit if a guy came by the house in a car and I stood by the car and talked to him. He didn't think it looked right—what would the neighbors think? I told my parents that Dean and I were just friends, and I knew they would be okay with that. I often wonder why they believed such a story. Many parents would not have fallen for that story.

When Mom and Dad were gone, I would invite Dean over to our house. Oh my, he was so personable, attentive, and affectionate. How lucky could I be? If only I had taken my time getting to know his true personality.

I went to the high school dances in town and would dance with some of Dean's friends from the army base. He didn't like to dance but had no problem with me dancing with his buddies. Life was good; I had finally found a way to enjoy my adolescence after feeling like my earlier childhood had been stolen from me. I was determined to make up for lost time.

By the time I was fifteen, my parents met Dean and allowed us to see each other with the condition that I would be home by ten o'clock at night. We spent most of our time together alone, and my parents did not realize how much we were involved. They trusted me. I do think my dad was suspicious of our relationship, but he didn't say anything at the time. I also think that Dad might have trusted Dean more because he was in the army. Dad had a very high regard for servicemen.

Dean had shared with me that he came from a family of six children in New Hampshire. They moved to Massachusetts when he was thirteen to live in the projects in Boston. Though he said his family got along well, all of the children were often left alone to do as they pleased without much supervision. His parents both worked different shifts to provide for the family. There was a lack of discipline, and the children were not given individual chores or responsibilities in the home other than his sister Kate. She helped out a lot with the house and the family. She always reminded me of myself and the responsibilities that I had at home. She also left home at a very young age and is still happily married to the same man today.

Dean didn't have any particular responsibilities and just hung out with his friends. He had a lot of freedom and eventually got into trouble with some of his friends. At the age of seventeen, he was told by a judge to either go into the army or go to jail, so at the tender age of seventeen, he dropped out of school and joined the service with some of his friends. I should have gotten a clue about Dean right then as a young man who had been in trouble with the law so young and had quit school to enter the military.

Dean's upbringing sounded light-years better than mine. He received letters from his parents often, and they appeared to support him in anything he wanted to do. My fondness for him continued to grow as we figured out ways to spend more time together.

I had been forced to be the surrogate mother to several children and spent my time cleaning house, listening to my mother's woes, and playing referee between my parents. The only thing important to me at that time was to have fun, regardless of the consequences. Since I was a small girl, all I ever dreamed about was to have my own home and a family of my own—a very different family from what I knew. Mine would be a marriage of mutual respect and trust, and Dean seemed like he would be a great dad and husband. Ah, so much for the common sense of a teenager.

Today, I do believe that I had been looking for someone who cared about me unconditionally—someone who would support my goals and believed that I was worth more than babysitting, cleaning, breaking up fights, and being a go-between. I fell head over heels for Dean, and we talked often about getting married and having children. That is all I really wanted at that time—to get married, have children, own a decent house, and live happily ever after. How naïve we are when young. Being patient and waiting for the right person to come along is not on our radar. It certainly wasn't in mine.

Chapter 3

We Are Determined to Do as We Want

My parents would let me see Dean once in a while, but our time together was very limited. I had a ten o'clock curfew, and Dean had to depend on his friends for rides to see me because he did not have a car at the time. I would ask Dean to come over when I was babysitting for other people. I would sneak him in the back door and out before the people came home. I remember sitting for the people across the street from our home and doing this same thing. I am surprised I didn't get caught. I think Mom thought because it was right across the street she would have noticed something. How sneaky we can be as kids.

My parents did not know, but we had sex before they had ever met him. I did whatever I had to do to see him. I skipped school a couple of times and went to one of his friend's home to spend the day with him. His friend was married and had a little girl. We would babysit for them while they went out so we could spend the time together. By the summer of 1962, Dean received orders to go overseas. He had put in a request before we met to be assigned time overseas. Needless to say, I was very upset. He assured me that everything would work out, and we would be together. We both agreed that we wanted to have children, so we tried to get pregnant.

He left to go overseas, and shortly after, I found out we had succeeded. I had missed my period and knew that I was probably pregnant at fifteen and alone. There was so much that happened when I left home that I often felt my brother and sisters resented me for creating so many problems in the family. We cannot control the reaction of our parents when they learn about circumstances that we cause in our lives. Often the ones who are left behind get the brunt of the outcome.

The fact that I had gotten pregnant caused a lot of havoc in the family. Mom and Dad had enough problems before this happened. At first, I kept the news to myself. I started a letter to Dean telling him that I was pregnant, but I ended up tearing it apart and throwing it in the bathroom garbage. I had not expected my mom to find it and piece it together. Mothers have this sixth sense; they somehow just know when things aren't right.

It was only about two days after I'd thrown the letter in the garbage that my mom confronted me. After coming home from school, Mom asked me if I was indeed pregnant. She said if I was not pregnant, there was no need to involve my dad. We both knew that the mother of all arguments would ensue. I told Mom that I thought I was pregnant but had not been to a doctor to confirm it. We were both deeply afraid of Dad's reaction, thinking he would go off the deep end.

Teenagers are not capable of thinking beyond their noses when they want something so much. I wanted a baby, a husband, and my own home far away from the daily fighting. I had never stopped to think about the consequences past that desire—for example, where I would go. I was afraid of my dad's reaction and decided to run away. Where I would go was not even a thought. I called my friend Melba, and she picked me up on her way to the movies. I didn't want to go to the movie, so I spent the entire evening hiding in her car. I remember being afraid that my dad would find me, so I would hide every time a car would go by. When Melba came back to the car, I knew that I could not run away. I had nowhere to go. I went to a Western Union and sent a cable to Dean. It simply read: "Help. I'm pregnant."

After playing out various scenarios, I went home to face the music. There was no other good choice. It was everything but harmony once Dad found out. He blew up like a tsunami hitting land. He wanted me to give up the baby for adoption. Dean received my cable and called my dad, who was not at all receptive to what Dean had to say. We wanted to get married as soon as possible so we could begin our new life and look forward to having our first child. But Dad stood his ground and would not approve of a marriage or keeping our baby. Keeping the baby was one decision that was not his to make. He could keep me from getting married because I needed his consent. My mother could have done it, but there was no way she was going to do that. The price would have been too high.

One of the things that upset me was that my father called my grandma Mildred as soon as he found out I was pregnant and told her. Dad knew this would upset me and also my mother. He said, "Look what your granddaughter has done now. She is pregnant."

Grandma supported me, and I was confident that she didn't think less of me because I was pregnant. I always knew she loved me no matter what. This is unconditional love as far as I am concerned. This was great for me, because I needed the reassurance that she cared. When my daughter Kim was a baby and Grandma was close to dying, she had a baby shower for me and sent the clothes for Kim home with my mom. Kim and I were not able to attend the shower, because flights were too expensive and we could not afford the trip. I last saw her when Kim was a year old, and she got to hold her first great-grandchild. I remember that when we were leaving, I cried because of the feeling that it would be the last time we would see one another. It was.

I was about two months pregnant when Dad finally calmed down a bit. They decided to take me to see our local priest. I was attending school and in the first semester of the tenth grade. I didn't talk to my brother and sisters about the situation, and we all tried to live as normally as possible. It was time for our appointment with the parish priest. I had never met him, and

I definitely knew my dad never had either. Mom made sure we went to church on Sundays, but dad rarely went.

The priest discussed the situation with the three of us, and they all agreed that I would go to the Catholic unwed mothers' home hundreds of miles away and give my child up for adoption. I felt that to keep peace in the family it was the best for me to agree to go until I could figure out what else to do. I signed the paper so they would accept me at the unwed mothers' home, and everyone was satisfied. They explained to me that whoever adopted my baby would pay for everything, and while at the home, I would be expected to work cleaning, etc. We went home, and things were quiet and normal for a while.

I continued to go to school and was not allowed to communicate with Dean at all. Dean mailed letters to a friend's house, and she would get them to me. My friend Lois helped me a lot at that time. That is how we communicated for the next couple of months. I let Dean know what was going on and knew that he wanted to get married as soon as we could. At least for now, everyone had calmed down thinking that I was agreeable to giving up my baby. Dean was sending letters to Lois's house, and we were trying to figure out what to do. Dean told his parents what was happening, and they were very supportive. They suggested that I go to their home and stay until he could return from overseas. At that time, this was not something I could make happen.

Thanksgiving and Christmas passed with the normal family events, and my parents pretended everything was normal. Dad had calmed down a lot, and they were not fighting as much. I will say my dad was always calmer and happier around the Christmas holiday. It was always a holiday that he enjoyed, and he did not seem to drink too much or get angry. My parents even had their normal New Year's Eve party. My brother and sisters were happy and thought everything was okay except I looked like I was putting on a lot of weight. It was early in my pregnancy but I was putting on the weight too fast.

After Christmas, the priest called. He told my mom that they had room and I could leave for the unwed mothers' home. I had just gotten home from school when Mom told me the unwed mothers' home was ready to take me in. I told her that I was not going to go. Trouble really started after that.

I dropped out of school at the end of January; by that time I was showing too much, and everyone knew what was going on. At that time, it was not acceptable for pregnant girls to attend school. The rumor mill was spinning, and girls like me had bad reputations. A young, pregnant, single girl had quite a stigma. My dad went nuts when Mom told him I was not going away. He raised cane with me and sent me down to the basement to sleep by myself. He told me to stay there and not come up for any reason.

The basement had an apartment on one side that two young women rented from the owner of the house. The other side, where I stayed, was a normal cement basement with tiny windows and a bed. I was afraid of what Dad would do and of being alone. Remember, I was the one who would sleep between my two sisters. I was afraid of the dark and felt trapped and isolated. I could hear the girls next door when they came home and became a bit comforted that they were on the other side of the wall. They didn't know what was happening in our home, but I wonder how much they really heard. The walls were thin, and there was certainly a lot of hell raising going on then. During the day, I would sit at the top of the stairs and be ready to hurry back downstairs in case Dad came home. It was a lousy life, and I was feeling the results of my actions.

I snuck upstairs one morning, called the district attorney's office, and told them what was going on. Don't ask me where I got that idea. I was just looking for help. They eventually called my parents and had the three of us go down to talk to them. They talked to me about my situation with Dean and how involved we were when we were together. I often felt that my parents may have been listening when I was questioned by them. I gave them many details about our relationship and told them that I would never press charges against Dean as my parents wanted. They talked to my parents and me and then advised my dad to take me home and support me. When we got home, he told me to go the basement, and I did.

He got worse and drank more. Mom called the police that night, and they were going to take him downtown to jail. This brought back old memories, but I thought they would at least keep him overnight. Instead, they let him go, and he came back home. Dad came in, saw me upstairs, and told me to go downstairs where the rest of the dogs belonged. I didn't have much contact with the family after that. By that time, I was three months pregnant and had spent a couple of weeks in the basement. I had no contact with my friends or letters from Dean.

One night Dad came home drunk and kept my mom up all night, yelling and carrying on. I am sure my brother and sisters were also awake. He threw dishes and all kinds of things all night long. The next morning my mom came down and said, "I have to get you out of here." I had crushed their dreams for me.

According to Mom, Dad said that Dean was "a no-good broom sweeper." If Dean had been an officer in the marines, Dad might have liked him. Or if Dean had put more effort into learning a trade while he was in the army, Dad might have approved. But Dean's job was in maintenance, cleaning up roads after the snow, plowing, and keeping the grounds looking nice—not much preparation for the future to be able to support a family. My parents also had aspirations of me graduating and making something of myself. Because I had to quit school, they felt I would not accomplish much success in life. I was determined to have a good life, and I knew that meant helping to take care of my children. I believed I would succeed but had bigger problems at the time.

My mother arranged for me to stay with a couple whom I had babysat for. The husband agreed to let me stay as long as I helped his wife with the kids at home and him at his store. I liked the woman, and she was very nice to me while I stayed at their home. He was a bit strange and more interested in my working off room and board by helping him with his business. I had grown up to be very independent and had no problem helping the family out by taking care of the children and doing some housework. I worked at his store and followed their rules while I was with them.

Depression was never a problem. I just did what I felt I had to do day in and day out—sometimes like a robot. They lived a couple of blocks away from our home. It was strange to see my brother and sisters come and go, but I couldn't let them know where I was staying. I felt like I was always hiding from Dad—just like when my mom left my dad and the car broke down in front of the house or when we hid in the bedroom at my cousins' house.

After staying with this couple for a week or so, my mom called and said the district attorney's office had found a place for me to go and stay. As I got older, I found out that Mom had called them and asked for help.

Life at home was terribly chaotic, and I found no support whatsoever from my dad. Mom had a hard time dealing with him and taking care of the rest of the kids. There was too much turmoil for everyone. Accepting the inevitable was the best choice for me and the rest of the family.

Dean's parents had told him that I could come to their home and stay until he returned. Being only fifteen, my parents would never have approved of this. Dad had no idea where I was staying, and Mom just wanted to find a placed for me that was safe. Mom took me to the bus; I kissed her good-bye and left for an unwed mothers' home on the other side of the state. It was hard saying good-bye to her. I knew she was very upset with my situation and wanted to help me as much as possible. I had no idea where I was going but ended up in a town that I knew nothing about and where I did not know anyone. It took hours by bus to arrive, and I was worried about the kind of place this would be. I didn't have much information about the unwed mothers' home, but I knew I had to go there. I did know that the home was run by the Lutheran church, and I did not have to sign my baby away to stay there.

A lady named Marion met me at the bus station and took me to the home where I would stay for five months. She was such a nice lady and very supportive. She ended up being my social worker while I was at the home, and over the years, I have continued to communicate with her. Once I met Marion, I felt much more comfortable about being there. It was a very modern and nice place.

Many women or young girls ranging in age from thirteen to thirty lived at the home. Two girls shared each room, and we all had common areas to meet for meals, socializing, and playing cards or other games. We each had responsibilities for cleaning our own rooms, and a rotation was put in place each week for cleaning the common areas. Everyone pitched in and helped one another. A cook took care of all the meals, and we would all sit together for lunch and dinner at a huge, long table in the dining room. It felt much like a home and, in most cases, was very peaceful. Once in a while some of the ladies would get into an argument, but the women in charge quickly handled the situations. It felt very safe even though all of us were strangers and came from different environments. We all had one thing in common—we all needed a home until our babies were born.

Each Monday we all trucked up to the hospital for our weekly physicals, and the current medical residents would take care of us. It was very uncomfortable for me to have four or five guys there while I was getting an internal exam with my legs spread-eagle. They were young residents, and I was the person who was needy, as well as their guinea pig. They were all nice, but I was humiliated to have to show my private parts so openly. It was embarrassing for all of us, but we needed the medical treatment and it was provided by the state.

The home was in a small town on the other side of the state, and we were located a few blocks from the downtown area. The people in the town knew about the Summit Home, and when we would go into town, it seemed they knew who we were. Maybe it was just our imagination, but when a bunch of pregnant girls are walking together into town, it seemed obvious to me that they would know we were from the home. We often went into town to see a show or get an ice cream and assumed that people knew we were from "the home." I didn't care what they said or thought. I just ignored them. Each of us was told the hours we could be away, and there was a curfew for all of us to be home. In the evenings, a woman stayed with us to ensure everything was okay and to take anyone who may go into labor to the hospital. The hospital was close-by, so we were only left alone for a short time.

One night a guy was seen looking in the windows on the second floor, and one of the girls starting screaming. We were alone because the housemother had gone to the hospital. While the girls became hysterical and afraid, I told them to keep quiet and went to the office and called the police. It was no big deal. I was used to it. It was funny that being one of the youngest, I was the one to call the police. The police came and checked things out, and everyone was fine.

After a young woman had her baby, the church arranged for the adoption. I don't know if the adoptive parents paid any of the expenses. I assume they must have, because it was all arranged. After the birth, you were not allowed to see or hold your baby, because the people handling the adoptions thought this was best for the mother. The mother came back to the home, signed the adoption papers, gathered her things, and left.

All the girls had different stories about getting pregnant and the father of their children. I saw many girls leave and cry terribly because they could not keep their children. It had to be devastating to give birth to a tiny human being who had grown within you for nine months after feeling it move and take on a life all its own only to never see it and then have to give it up to strangers. I was the first girl to leave the home and keep my baby.

All of the people working at the home were very nice and supportive of us. We played cards; I learned to crochet baby booties and blankets. When the girls would get to crying and fretting over their situations, I would encourage them and start a game for all of us to play.

All of us had one thing in common—our pregnancies—so we all got along well and pitched in to keep our home neat and support one another. We had an opportunity to make a little extra money by working for families in the area. I had a couple of jobs cleaning house and ironing. It helped out having some money to go to a movie or buy something for myself.

In the meantime, things were very difficult for my mom, brother, and sisters at home. The arguing continued, and from what I learned later, Dad shot a hole through the roof of the house one evening. I guess Mom and Dad were having a big argument about me, and Dad decided he wanted to shoot Dean. Of course, Dean was overseas, but I guess that wasn't the point for my dad. He was scaring Mom and my brother and sisters with the guns again.

I talked to my mom once in a while, and she would write me and enclose a few dollars for me to have some spending money. Dad and I did not have any communication at all. Dean and I continued to write letters, and he came home on leave from overseas to marry me. He took various flights and went home to his parents first. He then flew to the closest base and hitchhiked to where I was staying. Dad would not approve of our getting married, so after visiting for a day, he returned overseas. We then planned for me to go stay with his parents after I had the baby.

When I was eight months pregnant, my father finally called and said I could marry Dean. He wanted me to live with them while Dean was overseas. Mom, Dad, and my brother and sisters had all moved to California while I was in the home. Dad had found a better job in a nicer place. I wanted to save money, so I took a bus instead of a plane and went to California. By the time I arrived, I had blown up like a balloon. I could hardly find my swollen ankles, but I could sure feel them. My sister Susan told me that when I first walked into the house, they finally knew what all the raucous had been about. Until then, they didn't know what had happened to me or that I was pregnant.

I do not know exactly why my father changed his mind about Dean and me getting married. Mom must have talked to him and softened his attitude. There was nothing he could do about my pregnancy, and he knew I was determined to keep the baby at any cost. Dad told me to come home to finish out the pregnancy and have the baby there. It was a relief for me. However, I was afraid the arguments and throwing things in a rage would still be the norm at home.

Dean came home on leave from Okinawa for four days so we could marry. On August 3, 1963, we became husband and wife. We could not marry on such short notice in the Catholic church. I finally found a Lutheran minister who would marry us, and that is where we went. The minister and his wife were very nice to us, especially in our circumstances. The friends of Dean's we had babysat for while we were dating in North Dakota had also moved to California. They ended up standing up for us at ten o'clock that night, and we were married. After the short ceremony, we returned to my parents' house. At eight months pregnant, I was exhausted but finally married. My parents did their best when we got back home. They had made up the couch for us in the living room; that was where we spent our first night as husband and wife.

My five siblings were constantly around, which meant the house was always in chaos without opportunity to be alone. The next night we went to the drive-in to have a little fun and spend some private time together. Once Dean left for Okinawa again, I had a hard time adjusting and waiting to have our baby. Mom and Dad started their usual fighting one weekend, and it was too much for me. In the middle of night, while they raged on, I left and started walking up the street. I had no idea where I was going or how I would get there. I just didn't want to live in that type of environment again. Mom got in the car and came down the street to pick me up and take me home. I went back because in the middle of the night and alone, my alternatives were limited.

My worries about the drunken fights continuing had merit. When I returned to the house, Dad sat me on his lap and said that as long as I was there the fighting would stop. He kept his promise, and the house was quiet for the next year. I don't know how they managed to do it. What I do know is that the fighting and arguing had been reduced a great deal, and I was thankful.

My due date came and went. A week later, after cleaning all of the floors, I began having pains. They often say that a woman becomes very energetic and does a lot of cleaning just before she goes into labor. In my case, it was true. Keeping it quiet, I kept track of how often the contractions came. We were all in the living room watching TV when my dad asked, "How long have you been in labor?" How did he know? I guess that after six children, he would know. I told him seven hours. Mom panicked and made me nervous. She wanted to call the doctor right away. After awhile, she made me so paranoid that I agreed to go to the hospital.

Dad got me into the car, and off we went. I did not know if he was stressed or excited, but he passed up the parking lot and drove the car onto the grass at the front door of the hospital. My parents were not allowed to be with me at all. We got there at eight o'clock that night, and after a long, arduous labor, I had Kim at noon the next day. I felt so alone and had a picture of Dean next to me. I had my baby daughter naturally, which was not easy for a sixteen-year-old.

We all went home after a week in the hospital, and my sisters Susan and Lauren helped me care for my newborn Kim. Life went on, and taking care of a baby was quite a job. I am thankful to my sisters and mother for helping me out. My mother would hear Kim crying at night and wake me up. I was a very sound sleeper and would not hear her crying. Think about it—I was a teenager and not used to that type of responsibility. I took care of my brother and sisters, but Mom was the primary person responsible for their care, especially at night while everyone was asleep. Being a parent was quite an adjustment for me.

Dean and I wrote letters back and forth, and I decided to look for a job to make some money. I found a position as a babysitter for a single mom of a two-year-old and baby of a few months. Kim and I stayed at her house all week and went home on weekends. This lady knew how to take advantage of me by leaving early in the morning and not coming home until late at night. She loved to party after work, because she had a full-time, live-in babysitter. I felt sorry for her children, because they never saw their mom. I cleaned her house, fixed meals, and took care of her two kids plus Kim.

When I finally got tired of being alone all week, I told the lady that I was quitting to find a different job and stay with my parents. Kim and I stayed at home during the week, and I started looking for another job. Mom told me that she had received a call from a lady from Department of Children's Services, and the woman I babysat for had reported me for abusing her toddler. Mom supported me by taking me to DCS with Kim to talk to them. Such an accusation had the potential of ruining my life. I told them that a twelve-year-old girl who was a friend of this lady used to come to the house. She was often ornery with the toddler and ended up being hired after I had quit. The young girl later admitted to harming the toddler, and a retraction was put into the paper. I learned a big lesson about people from what happened in that situation. I realized that others can negatively affect my reputation, and I had to be careful to protect myself and my child.

Mom helped me a lot when it came to managing bills and getting out of some of my messes. She worked with Dad in his business taking care of the finances and was the primary person in our family to manage the bills. This was quite a tough job for her, because she did not have complete control over how the money was spent. Mom and Dad had many financial problems, and she would get jobs working as a waitress at local restaurants and country clubs. People really liked her on the job. She was very personable and really understood the catering business.

She later worked managing boys that delivered newspapers. The boys really loved her and missed her after she quit her job. Mom felt she had to make more money because Dad liked to spend on hobbies. He liked all the newest electronics, especially anything related to cameras, computers, or technical equipment. I think he had a vision of starting up another business and thought purchasing that type of stuff could be a way of the future.

Mom understood this but also knew the bills had to be paid. She would often hide money so he didn't spend it. At that time, such equipment was very costly. I think Mom often had to lie to him about the finances so he couldn't spend the money she'd hidden.

I knew it was costing them a lot to take care of Kim and me while Dean was away. I was trying to save for Dean's return. Because he was in the service, I knew we would be moving away and I needed to find work until he came home.

Chapter 4

Decisions We Make That Impact Our Lives

When Dean came home to marry me—when I was eight months pregnant with Kim, blown up like the Hindenburg, and miserable—we'd had a serious discussion. We had just gotten married and were talking about the next year when he would be back overseas. He was returning to Okinawa for another year and would have an opportunity to go on leave for R&R (also known as rest and relaxation) to Japan. He wanted to know if it would be all right if he took advantage of the availability to have sex with someone else. His question was such a shock to me that I started to cry.

We had just gotten married, and I had already been through so much. His wanting to have my permission to have one-night stands sent me over the edge. With no good way to solve the dilemma, we dropped the subject. He did not understand that with marriage was supposed to come loyalty and trust. Once that is broken, things are never the same again. But to Dean it was just an opportunity to release his sexual frustrations because I could not be with him. I was eight months pregnant and had gone through so much to be with him that I expected him to use self-control while we were apart. I think most young women would think the same. The bonds of marriage are sacred and meant to be taken seriously. We made promises to respect and be loyal to each other. Evidently, Dean had not taken those commitments as seriously as I had. I was disappointed in a big way, but what could I do? Dean thought of himself as quite the playboy, which, consequently, destroyed my trust in him.

I eventually found a job at A&W working inside and took another babysitting job up the street. Rob was a single father with two sons. He was twenty-seven, and I was sixteen. I had Kim with me and cleaned the house and fixed meals while I babysat. Rob knew a good deal when he saw one coming. We became friends, and he gained my confidence enough for me to tell him about issues that were troubling to me. Through time, I told him about Dean's asking about going on R&R, and of course, he gave me his opinion that Dean was having sex with other women.

I tried to believe that Dean understood how much it had upset me to think about him having sex with other women, and I hoped he would reconsider. About two months before Dean was to come home from overseas, he went on an R&R. I could tell from his letters he had been fooling around. The words he used made me realize something wasn't right. Rob assured me that Dean certainly had his flings. In hindsight, I should have known Rob's agenda but was too young and vulnerable at the time to see it. I never talked to my mom or anyone about Dean's possible infidelity or Rob's responses and kept things to myself. One evening things went too far, and I became sexually involved with Rob. I then started going to parties with a girl named Bonnie whom I worked with at A&W. I would go out in the evening, and my parents would watch Kim. I met lots of guys but steered clear of any sexual relations. I always thought that if I wanted sex, I could go see Rob.

I met Tony at one of Bonnie's parties, and he was a very nice guy. He invited Bonnie, her boyfriend, and me over to his home for dinner one evening. He had a beautiful home, and we had a wonderful time together and a great dinner. It was very nice. As I think back, I don't know what I was thinking at the time. I was married and going out on dates. The distance I felt between Dean and I was incredible. I felt like I didn't know him anymore. Tony tried to talk me into not going back with

Dean when he returned. The guy was very nice, but I wasn't interested. At the same time, I was not too keen on going with Dean when he got home. I felt things had changed a lot between us, and I was right about that.

The gap grew further during the next six weeks before he came home. One evening Dean showed up at the door two weeks early. I was surprised. I had made plans with Rob for the next day and called to say I would not be able to "babysit." Rob owed me money for sitting for the kids, so I stupidly took Dean to his house and introduced them. I had absolutely no intention of ever telling him about my relationship with Rob. How stupid and naïve we are at that young age. Needless to say, I was very confused about everything by that time. I had a daughter and needed to be there for her. I also thought she would need her dad in her life.

Dean told me right away that he had gone on R&R and had been with another woman. I think he assumed I'd been faithful to him.

Chapter 5

We Are Now on to Our Life Together

Dean and I only had a couple of months of wedded bliss. Dean came home in May, and we traveled across the country to visit his family. Kim was ten months old and was getting to know her dad for the first time. We really enjoyed ourselves on that trip. We stopped in Michigan, and I was able to see my grandmother for the last time before she died. She got to see Kim and hold my little girl, and this was a wonderful thing for me. We traveled from Michigan to Massachusetts, and I met Dean's family for the first time. They were very nice people. The day we got there his mother was at work, and his dad called her to come home and see us. It was a big deal for Dean to be coming home, and his family sure made a big deal out of it. He was truly the apple of his mom's eye, and his dad was pretty proud of him as well. We spent about a month visiting his family and went on a trip to New Hampshire to visit his grandmother, aunts, and cousins. Dean was close to his grandmother as well. She was a very nice lady, and I think that our trip may have been the last time he was able to visit with her.

Dean's family was close and did a lot to help each other out. After spending a lot of good time together, we left Massachusetts and headed for our new home at an army base in Kentucky. Dean had extended his service for another three years. This gave him a chance to find a better job on the outside. Dean's parents had given us some money for our wedding, which helped us out quite a bit when we arrived in Kentucky.

We needed to find a rental quickly, because we had no place to stay. Not being familiar at all with the area, we looked in the paper and found rentals. We ended up renting the basement of a very nice house for a decent price—at least one we could afford. This was our first home together, so it was exciting. The house was fairly new, and the upstairs apartment was great. Our basement apartment, however, left a lot to be desired.

We did not have any furniture, so we rented it already furnished—if you could say that. The floors were the typical basement cement except for the carpet in the bedroom. The bathroom had part of a fence on the floor that we would stand on to take a shower. There was no sink in the bathroom, so we used the sink in the kitchen for everything. When the storms came and it rained, water rushed down the walls in the living room and got everything wet. The entire apartment continually had a musty smell and the bugs that come with a wet basement. There was a bar in the kitchen that was made of plywood and not much at all. Dean decided to replace the bar with a good structure to improve the place. He was very handy and did a great job of making it nicer. There wasn't much you could do with the rest of the place. It just gave us incentive to move into something better. Still, for us, it was home.

It was about the middle of July when we decided to go to the local church and have our marriage blessed. I had been brought up in a Catholic environment, and we were taught that if you were not married in the church, you weren't married. You could not go to communion, and according to the church, we were living in sin. As such a young girl, I believed this to be true and wanted to make things right. Also being a Catholic, Dean had no problem with this. My parents wanted us to wait longer, but I did not listen. We had to go see the priest like most people do before getting married for a number of visits before they would marry us. We went to one of our normal visits, and I began to realize the big mistake that I had made while Dean was overseas. I felt guilty and knew that I had to tell Dean about my infidelity before we got married in the church.

In the car on the way home, I told Dean that I'd had an affair while he was away and I was in California. That really ended a lot of the good times. When we arrived home, he asked a lot of questions, was visibly devastated, cried a lot, and went to bed. After that, things changed drastically in our relationship. Dean still wanted to get married, so we did in August of that year but things were never the same. People say that if you have an affair you should never tell the other person because you are just trying to rid yourself of the guilt. I don't know if this is true, because I could not live with myself forever knowing I'd had an affair. I had to tell, and that is who I am. Dean became angry and demanding in our relationship. It eventually led to his hitting me and trying to get information about my affair. He wanted all the details and would beat me up to get them. I found myself saying whatever I had to for him to finally stop. After he was satisfied with my answers, he would want to have sex. I was only seventeen years old at that time. I found it difficult to deal with his constant questioning and ridicule but knew I had to at the time.

I did the best I could to make a home for us, and we were about as happy as two people could be under the circumstances. Dean found part-time jobs to supplement his service salary, and life went on.

The result of having an affair with Rob became more evident to me. Dean was devastated and continued to want to know every little detail. I lied and told him basic stuff to minimize the hurt. Through time, he became obsessed and continued to hit me to get more information. He would put his hands around my neck and choke me until I could not breathe. I became very scared. I felt like I deserved to be punished, but at times, I did fear for my life. I went running up the road one day with Kim, and he picked me up and told me I was to go home or follow other demands and rules. I decided to go back to my parents' home. While we were headed to the airport, he said, "I don't want you to go." That started the roller coaster that was my life for the next twenty-three years. I believed that he wanted to make things right but didn't know how to at the time.

It became an everyday occurrence in our relationship that the questions of my relationship with Rob were always there. Dean wanted to know where we went, what we did during sex, and what I saw in Rob. It went on and on. Dean totally focused on this, and I thought his obsession was a bit crazy. What about the affairs he had when overseas? That did not seem to matter.

A wife was expected to remain faithful and true while the husband could do what he pleased. After all, he is a man with needs that the wife cannot always provide. Dean expected the house to always be clean and tidy, meals to be cooked and presented, and socks and underwear to be clean and organized in his drawer. He constantly reminded me of my duties as his wife. However, his duties consisted of doing whatever he wanted. When we visited with other couples, Dean could be a bit of a flirt, which was all right. At the same time, I had to be really careful of everything I said and did with other men. He was very jealous.

Dean would come home from work tired, hungry, and ready for dinner. He would give Kim some attention, and she would be put to bed early. The evening time varied based on his mood. He could be very charming and nice, but if he was in a foul mood, he was demanding and angry. If angry, we would have an evening of abuse and name-calling, and questioning would start again. He would hit and choke me during his jealous temper fits. He would then want sex, and afterward, he'd become sorry and charming again.

Dean wanted sex every day and sometimes more. If I didn't feel like it or was too busy, he would insist and force me. It did not matter how much I fought him. I had no acceptable choice at that time. I felt trapped, but I had gotten myself into the situation and needed to deal with it. He would become sweet again with apologies flowing like good wine on a Sunday afternoon. Inevitably, the roughness would return, and I found myself caught up in this web of violence as Dean's normal way of living.

We finally decided to move from the basement apartment and bought a trailer. It was much nicer than the apartment, which was great for me. It was modern and clean and was our very own. Dean found a job working as a bartender at the Officers' Club. That brought in more money, and I got some part-time positions. We made some friends, and they thought we had such a good marriage. We would play cards and visit. It was a lie by that time, and I did a great job of covering things up. I never admitted to anyone, including my family, that we had any problems in our marriage.

By that time, Kim was one year old, and I was expecting again. I knew I was in the relationship for my lifetime and wanted to make it work. When a young girl wants nothing more than to be married, have children, and live happily ever after, it rarely happens. The brain has not matured enough to acquire good common sense and the ability to read people beyond what is said and how they appear. Living in a house with crazy parents and too much responsibility at a young age can cause a girl to fantasize about the grass being greener elsewhere. There are always weeds and thorns among the green grass no matter what the family situation may be. It is important to learn to bloom where you are planted and to gain the skills necessary to make decisions that will help you grow.

I truly believed that my marriage would be an example of true love and respect. If I would have stopped and used common sense by keeping my eyes wide open, I would have left Dean at that time. I knew he had lost respect for me, and I was in an abusive relationship. In 1964, I was seventeen and pregnant with our second child.

I clung to Dean because of the situation at my parents' home. I had been tired of living with near constant anger and fear and enduring the fighting, breaking things, and tearing down of doors. I had become weary of my home life and constantly taking care of my siblings. The easiest way out was to meet someone, get married, and live happily ever after. Dean sure seemed like a guy I would have liked to spend my life with.

I was very young and had not been taught important dynamics to strengthen my perception or to listen to my inner voice; instead, I just knew I had to survive. It is possible to learn how to survive at a young age whether you are taught by your parents or not. I had not learned to take my time when I meet someone and get to know the person first, having serious conversations about what I wanted out of a relationship, as well as my expectations. Make sure you have a lot in common, because the days will get stressful and you need to get out and have some fun-loving times together. To do otherwise is to throw yourself to the wolves. No one will ever take better care of you than you can.

Chapter 6

Trying to
Build a Life Together

My relationship with Dean grew more complicated as time went on. I was pregnant with David and needed to get a job to help support the family. I eventually got a job as a waitress but was let go after the first day. I wasn't friendly enough I was told. Actually, I didn't understand enough about working as a waitress and did not want to make any mistakes. I concentrated so much on what I was supposed to do that I appeared unfriendly. I then found a job working in a dry cleaning business. Kim stayed with a babysitter during the day while I worked. Dean was gone a lot of evenings with his bartending job. When I was about seven months pregnant, I had to quit my job, because it was tough carrying the heavy bags of laundry at that time.

I made many friends in the trailer park in the short time we were there. Most of them were stationed on the base and around our age. We had a lot in common, because a few of us were pregnant at the same time. I think Dean was not as violent because of my pregnancy. He pushed me a few times and would just demand sex when he wanted it.

It was a tough pregnancy with all of this going on, and Kim was a handful. She had received a lot of attention when we lived with my family in California. She was not used to being with just her father and me; plus, she was used to being the center of attention all the time. I did the best I could.

While visiting a girlfriend of mine one day, I went into labor. She took care of Kim while Dean took me to the hospital. Unfortunately, he could not come into the labor or delivery room while I gave birth to our son. Things were different back then, and the hospitals were very strict about allowing anyone in while a woman was giving birth. There was a young girl in labor the same room that I was in, and she kept yelling and carrying on at the time. She would not stay covered up, so the hospital would not let Dean come in to see me. Our son David was an easy labor for me, and we were very proud of our new son. We now had two beautiful children—a daughter and a son. What could be better? I hoped that things would change, and we could have a good life together.

It was not to be so. Eventually, life returned to the arguing and abuse. I sheltered Kim and David the best I could during those times. I did not want to repeat my own childhood where my mother involved me in everything between her and my dad. I had known too much back then, and it affected how I felt about my father and my perceptions about the world. I did not want that to happen to my children.

When growing up at home, I learned that our family had many different times together. It may be fun and happy or at times crazy and angry. Though kids may not like what is going on in the family, they are still learning subconsciously, and the teachings carry on throughout their lifetime.

I did my best teaching my children right from wrong, despite Dean's ridiculous beliefs and refusal to see anything differently. When two parents are at odds about how to raise children, it causes confusion. Children look at the two opposite ways of parenting and will usually choose the easiest as their life path. With no career to fall back on so I could become independent from Dean, all I could do was teach my children the best way I knew and hope for the best. Today, I truly believe that I did all I possibly could to raise them right.

I finally relented and just went along with Dean's terribly abusive nature in order to keep the house as peaceful as possible for my children. I had no career and nowhere else to go except home with my parents, and that was not happening. My brother Jerry says today that I stayed with Dean to spite our dad. He thinks I didn't want Dad to be right in the end. Maybe that's true—who knows?

After having David, I got a job at another cleaners taking in laundry and working the front desk. My supervisor came to me one day and said someone had complained that I was not being friendly enough. I thought I tried to keep things moving to get rid of the lines. This was one of my first experiences dealing with politics. I had to slow down and say, "Hello. How are you, and how is your day?" Oh well, forget the lines. After a period of time, the supervisor told me that the person who had complained said I was doing much better. It was a learning experience for me. Always show a smile and appear to care about the customers who are always right.

Dean's bad attitude wore on me greatly. Taking care of two small children; doing all of the housework, laundry, cooking, shopping, and errands; working at the cleaners; and paying the bills became exhausting. Dean decided he wanted to move close to his parents' home so he could see his family more often. He put in for a transfer, and in a short amount of time, he got one. We were being transferred to upstate New York, and that meant being able to travel to see his family over a weekend. He was happy with the transfer, and I thought it might work out for the best.

Shortly before leaving, we had a car accident, and I ended up in the hospital for X-rays because of my injuries. It appeared that everyone was okay, and we just had to find another car to drive east because ours was totaled. We didn't really have enough money but managed to find a car that might be able to make it to his home in Massachusetts. That would make for a nervous trip with a car that may not make it. The service was moving our trailer to the new base, and just before we left, the base hospital called and asked me to come in and see them.

They told me I had a tumor that would have to be removed surgically. I had to leave, so they gave me a letter to carry with me in case there was a problem; they were concerned that the tumor could rupture. I was to have it taken care of as soon as we arrived at our next base. I thought the car problem was bad, but worrying about a physical problem added more stress. I quit my job at the cleaners, and we headed east.

Chapter 7

Still Trying to Make It Work

Kim was three years old and David a year old when we left Kentucky and headed for upstate New York. We found a nice trailer park with a nice pool. It was winter at the time, but summer would be great for the kids. It was nice for the kids, because their home was the same but in a different location. They were so young that they hardly knew the difference.

We went to visit Dean's family before settling in and mentioned the fact that I had to go to the hospital for surgery. I thought I would be spending a week in the hospital and a few weeks recovering. Dean had to work, and we needed someone to stay with the children. My sister-in-law, Jen, was a single mother and moved in with us with her two little children. She took care of the four kids and tried to maintain the trailer while I was in the hospital. I ended up having to stay in the hospital for two weeks, which was tough on her. It was difficult for all of us living in a two-bedroom trailer with four kids and three adults, but we did it.

Dean criticized Jen because she went out too much, and he didn't care for the jobs she found. Most of them were working evenings at the bars, but that's what she found available at the time. I have to give her credit; other girls at that time would have stayed home and not worked at all. Living all together only worked for a short time before she went back home. Dean could be very critical and expected her to live like he thought she should. She was very independent and would do as she pleased. Jen and I got along well, but her brother was a pain for both of us.

Dean did not like the job he had in New York—just like Kentucky. He worked with some people who could have him transferred to another base. He wanted to go to a place where he could get a better education and career for our future, so we left New York and went south. The trailer went with us.

It was hot, and we didn't have any extra money. I got a job at a dry cleaners working sixty hours a week at a dollar an hour and was paying fifteen dollars of my paycheck to a day-care center. I did this for a couple of months and decided there had to be a better way. Getting an education for a better work environment and making more money was necessary. I had to think about a career, as I was getting older and needed to support my children and be more independent. A part-time position opened up at a department store, so I took that and enrolled in a business college. I had visions of being a secretary one day, which was considered a good career choice in those days. I found a babysitter to come over when I worked, and Dean took care of the kids in the evening so I could take night courses. One of the first courses I took was typing and accounting. After two courses in typing, I took a keypunch course.

During this time, Dean was very difficult. He would hit me, kick me, and hold me down on the floor by my throat. I would feel like I was passing out, and at the last moment, he would let go. I tried to keep quiet and not let the kids know what was going on. I guess because of my parents' noisy fights, I wanted to keep mine quiet. I made excuses for Dean, thinking that I deserved it. He also continued to be sexually abusive. He demanded sex and would hit me to get whatever he wanted. I cried, but he didn't care. He got what he wanted—or else.

One night I came home from work, and he was in a foul mood. The babysitter had taken care of the kids during the day, and I had gone to school after work. He was nasty and forced me to have sex. If I gave him a hard time, he hit me until I gave him want he wanted. I remember crying and feeling humiliated, but I dealt with the situation for the moment. Later, I learned that he'd had sex with the babysitter that day. I felt disgusted dealing in such a sick existence with a sex addict and a mean man.

We had only lived in the South for about a year when Dean's orders changed; we left the South and went north to Wisconsin. I had learned enough in school to get a job at the Base Exchange in the office. It was great that I could use my schooling to get a job for more money.

My grandpa came to visit, and my sister Lauren came up. Lauren was a nice person, quiet and sixteen years old. She came for the summer and babysat for the kids, which helped a lot and saved us a lot of money. She also kept the house clean and would help cook meals. It was a lonely environment for her, so she found a few friends and some entertainment.

The area was very rural with hardly anything to do. She would go out for an evening, but Dean didn't approve of her friends or her going out at all. I finally felt that my home was a bad environment for her even though I loved the company and enjoyed having someone from my family around. I called my dad's mom and asked her to come get Lauren and take her to visit with her for the rest of the summer. My grandma came north to get her, and Lauren left. I was disappointed, because I enjoyed spending time with my sister.

I do believe that I did Lauren a favor by having my grandma come up and get her. We liked being around one another, but Dean made it difficult, and she was very frustrated about the situation. It was not a good time for her. She accepted the situation and left with my grandma. Dean had these ideas that he should dictate what girls did in life as if he was their universal, self-appointed boss and taskmaster. He did it with his sister Jen and now with my sister Lauren. I was not in a position to debate it with him. Lauren thought Dean was difficult, and I never told her about our problems.

Chapter 8

We Finally Were Settled in One Town

Kim was about five and David three when we left Wisconsin and headed east. Dean decided to leave the army and return to civilian life. We sold the trailer and bought a new car. Before leaving Wisconsin, we went to visit my Aunt Catherine and Uncle Dan in Michigan, and they helped us get a new car with some good financing.

We ended up moving to Newtown, Connecticut, and rented a crummy, furnished apartment and put the kids in day care. I got a job as a keypuncher at the same place Dean got a job as an electronics technician. Because we were working for the same company, it was easy for Dean to come into my department saying he was just visiting me. He was actually keeping an eye on me.

One afternoon I went out to lunch with two guys and a girl from my department, and Dean had a fit. I learned very quickly not to go out to lunch when it involved any men. This just gave him an excuse to accuse me of fooling around. He was super jealous and had lost all trust in me. I thought I could regain that trust; little did I know that would not happen. My trust in him was not even discussed. The chauvinistic world leaves a lot to be desired.

I worked hard to advance, and a position became available as a computer operator. I applied for the job, but the supervisor thought the job was more for a man because it required lifting heavy paper for the printers. I told him that I could lift the boxes and wanted the opportunity. He gave me the chance, and I received a promotion. I loved the job and was good at it. It was a good opportunity for me to develop a career where I could make decent money.

After about a year, I made the decision to quit work and stay home with the kids. They'd had a couple of bouts with some childhood illnesses, and staying out of work to take care for them was difficult. Companies were not very understanding in those days when it came to women working and having to take care of sick children. My boss once told me to call in sick for myself instead of the kids, because that was more acceptable.

Dean was so jealous. The stress of taking care of the kids, keeping the house in order, and dealing with him was too much for me. The pressure of Dean coming up to see me at work and always keeping an eye on me was very difficult. People whom I worked with were quite confused with his always appearing at my job, and I became weary of dealing with this situation. I had always wanted to be a wife and mother, and having a job or career was not that important.

Dean took up archery and was gone a lot of the time. I decided to take it up myself, and we could take the kids with us. The kids got tired of walking through the woods, but at least we were spending time together. We entered many archery tournaments and had some good times. It was a good opportunity to do things together as a family, but the reprieve from the arguments was short lived.

We were looking for a bigger apartment and saving to eventually purchase a home for ourselves. We found a nice place around the corner from where we lived, and the apartment was much larger and nicer. As renters, we always took care of the property like it was our own. We would paint, wallpaper, and make changes that improved the property for the owners.

We rented from a lady named Carol; she was very nice, and because I was home during the day, we became good friends. Carol was about twelve years older than me and had six kids. She would come downstairs and visit with me often. After watching me make spaghetti sauce using tomato soup, she decided I needed a few lessons. Carol was married to an Italian and knew how to make great sauce. She taught me to make sauce, and we spent a lot of time together. She always thought that I was controlled too much by my husband. She was right, but I would not admit it. She would come downstairs in the evening to visit with Dean and I. As he made his normal demands—get this, get that—she would say, "Get the fuck up and get it yourself!"

Dean often said Carol was a bad influence on me. He was afraid her attitude would rub off on me. But she was my savior. Carol became one of my best friends, and at that time, I surely needed a friend. I was never honest with her (or anyone else) about my marriage. Carol and I spent many days visiting with her friends or family and had a lot of fun together. She got me out with people, and I learned to have some fun just talking and laughing with others.

While renting from Carol, I decided to get involved at the school where Kim and David attended. Kim was in the second grade, and David was in kindergarten. I started taking on projects such as room mother and Brownie leader. I went to PTA meetings, and many of the women were quite a bit older than me. I was only twenty-one when Kim started school. They had their cliques, and I wasn't part of them. It made me realize that working for a living brought more respect and recognition than dealing with these busybodies. I decided to go back to work, because we needed the extra money and I would be much happier as well.

At this time in my life, many women criticized working mothers. I listened to their opinions and found myself defending myself as a working mother. Most of the women who did all the talking had husbands with good jobs and a nice home. They didn't have to worry about adding income to help the family out. Today, it's not a big deal, and it often takes more than one income to support a family.

I felt bad leaving the children at a nursery school all day. They needed more attention from their mom and dad than we gave them. We were caught up in our own problems, and they suffered because of that. Dean was not very attentive to the kids and was constantly criticizing David when he was very young. He would push him down, and when David cried, Dean would yell at him. I found this to be the actions of a man who was worried about his son being macho when he grew up. I did the best I could to defend David, although I wish I would have done more to defend him from his father's nasty disposition.

Dean and I decided to buy a home of our own and stop renting. After several attempts to obtain a mortgage, we finally found a two-family home with an owner who would work with us for the down payment. The downstairs had four rooms, and the upstairs apartment was rented out at the time. We thought the income from the apartment would help us make the payments.

The house needed a lot of work, but Dean was very handy at remodeling. We were thrilled to get our first home and moved into it with great hopes of making it a nice place to live. We were both working, the kids were in school, and the remodeling began. It seemed like we spent most nights working. Dean did the work, and I cleaned up the mess. We added a couple of rooms and were beginning to enjoy our new home.

I had found a job as a computer operator and worked to improve my profession plus make more money. My ultimate goal was to keep making more money to improve the lifestyle for our kids. Dean loved nice things—cars, boats, and motorcycles—and wanted an elaborate home. I kept the budget, paid the bills, got the loans, and tried to keep up with his need to buy toys. For example, when we were down south, he just had to have a rifle. It cost a lot of money at that time, but being so spoiled, he would live on the edge to get his playthings. I tried to conserve money while he bought what he wanted. It was like dealing with a spoiled kid who throws tantrums if he doesn't get what he wants. The difference here was that he was an adult—the tantrums were nastier.

It was through my job as a computer operator that I met Jim and Dora. Jim was my boss, and Dora was his wife. I met Dora for lunch one day, and we became friends forever. Dean didn't care much for Dora just like he hadn't liked Carol, because she was very opinionated. He didn't care much for women who stuck up for themselves; he felt that they needed to be beaten down and put back in their place.

Dean and I went places together over the years with Jim and Dora, plus we would get together for holidays and other times. None of us had family close-by for the holidays, so we spent some time together. There were many New Year's Eve parties to remember with them.

Dora and Jim had two children, and the younger son was disabled. He was born blind and was unable to develop to an adult level. He does have a remarkable skill of playing the piano naturally; he can hear music and play it. He was so gifted, and yet it was tough, especially for Dora. It took considerable time for her to work through her son's situation to ensure he could get the most out of life. Jim was very supportive and helped her a lot. Through time, they found the right program for him to develop in a good environment.

I worked for Jim for about eight years and continued my way up the career ladder. I went back to school at a technical college to take programming. I received an opportunity to become a programmer and jumped at the chance. It took a lot of reading technical manuals and relying on my manager for significant training. Our company was supported by IBM for their technical expertise at the time, and many engineers visited us for on-site consulting on a regular basis. I learned a tremendous amount from them that would lead me into my future positions at other companies. I had a tough job that required me to work 24/7 and weekends plus provide on-call support. It was not unusual to get called in the middle of the night and have to go into work.

I made decent money when we bought our first home, and as time passed, Dean wanted to buy another home in the neighborhood. We bought a two-family home and rented the apartments. I worried a lot about handling all of this financially, especially if tenants did not pay their rent. I also hated cleaning up after people who refused to take care of other people's property. Renters can be very demanding, and constant calls come in with problems to fix or their issues with other neighbors. It can be exhausting, especially when you have to chase them for the rent or get exterminators to come and get rid of the fleas from their animals. People often think when they rent that the landlords have it made because they are collecting money. It doesn't always work that way.

I called my mom, and she told me that my sister Lee was having problems at home. I didn't have a lot of information and told Mom to send her out to stay with Dean and me. Lee was sixteen years old, and I had a difficult time getting her into the local high school. I had to go to the superintendent of schools to get the approval for her to attend. I was determined to get her a fair chance and help her out. Lee was a beautiful girl and very vulnerable.

Dean turned on the charm around her and treated me like a queen. He did everything for me; you would have thought we were just the most loving couple. I should have known he had ulterior motives. Lee was lonely, and I think she wanted what I had. Little did she know what our relationship was really like.

Dean used to stay up later than me at night, and Lee would as well. One evening, I woke up and went downstairs. The two of them were lying on the couch, and he was feeling her up. I went nuts and put my sister on the first plane home. When Dean and I went upstairs, he gave me a bunch of excuses. I was so upset that I threw myself over the railing and down a flight of stairs. I ended up going to the hospital and told them that I'd accidentally fallen. I then realized that I did not want to die, and he wasn't worth it.

After that incident, my anger was dominant, and Dean got worse. His parents called one evening, and I told my father-in-law what was happening and that all this craziness was because I had gone out on him while he was overseas. My father-in-law said he had suspected something like that had happened. Dean went crazy when he discovered what I had told his father. He hung up the phone on his dad. When his mother called back, he hung up on her. He then dragged me by my hair up the stairs and knocked the crap out of me. The sad thing is that both kids watched as he dragged me upstairs.

That was the first time I had told anyone what was happening in my life. Dean had expected to keep his abusiveness a dark secret while on the outside we pretended to family and friends that our relationship was made in heaven. Such behavior is normal for abusive men, which is the epitome of dysfunction. They must appear as good, loving husbands or boyfriends, while inside the need to terrorize is an obsession that knows no bounds.

I believe that one of Dean's problems was a mental-health issue called narcissism. People who have this disease become selfish and self-thinking; if another person or situation does not, in some way, benefit the narcissist, he will do anything necessary to get what he wants. It doesn't matter if he has to become abusive in any manner to achieve his goal. The narcissist has no regard for any other human being other than himself. And there's nothing you can do about it except seek help from a professional, which Dean would never consider. Why would a perfect man need help? Dean truly believed he was perfect.

Things cooled down over time, and the craziness of our life together continued. I truly wanted a good family for my kids and wanted to make things work. We both had decent jobs, and the kids were getting older so we didn't need a babysitter. That freed up some cash, so we bought a piece of land and then a boat. Saving for a rainy day or for emergencies was out of the question. Dean wanted to live in a big house, to have fun with friends on our boat, and to build a home on our property.

Our relationship at the time was like a roller coaster—one of those love/hate type of relationships. Most people would have thought that we got along great, but people rarely know what goes on behind closed doors. Kim and David knew we had some arguments, but as I was taught as a young child, always try to keep the peace. In other words, keep the scams going no matter what. Before things got too loud and crazy, I would give in and perform. We had added a room upstairs for us. It was away from Kim and David, so when he knocked me around, it was not heard as easily. I tried to do most things he wanted to avoid these confrontations for the sake of my daughter and son.

Dean and I bought a nice boat and went out with a few friends on a regular basis to have a good time. I wasn't crazy about water, but the kids did enjoy it. It is surprising when you have a boat how many people gravitate toward you and act like they're your best friends, yet they take off as soon as you return to shore or go to the gas station.

I found myself responsible for fixing lunches for everyone when we went out. Dean had a habit of flirting with all the cute girls. He loved to upset me with that type of crap. Of course, I had to walk the line around other guys. He was very insecure and jealous.

When Kim and David were very young and Dean had gotten out of the service, we visited his parents. His brother Mark lived at home with their parents, and he was about my age. We were at their home visiting when Mark and I were talking upstairs in the bedroom. Dean walked in, and the two of them got into a fistfight that their parents had to stop. There was nothing going on except in Dean's imagination. I am sure Mark was confused and upset over his brother's reaction, but we never talked about it. Mark joined the service at about the same time and came home on leave a few years later, and everyone got along fine. He had completed his tour in Cambodia and returned to a base in the United States. We had him come to our home for a few days and stay with us. We visited, and things went well. We never talked about the incident that had happened years earlier.

Unfortunately, Mark passed away unexpectedly at the base. He had just been home on leave visiting all of us the year before and was waiting to be discharged. He had some minor surgery, and they said he died of heart failure. He was such nice guy and only in his early twenties; it was terrible that he died so young. He had so much more of life to live. It made me wonder how two different people from the same family could turn out so opposite.

During that terrible time, I do believe that I helped his family to arrange many of the details taking care of the arrangements for Mark's funeral. It was a very sad time for all of us. Losing a child at such a young age is devastating to a family. We all had to eventually get on with our lives.

I finally decided that I had to gain the skills and experience I needed to have a full-time career to support myself and my family. Sometimes after a devastating thing happens in your life, you consider changes and options. Finding a way to make a new and better life for me and my children was necessary, but I did not believe in divorce. Dean was always careful enough not to leave any obvious marks on my body when he decided to abuse me. This made the situation even worse. The big secret of his frequent abuse was getting harder to tolerate or hide. He was so good about treating me with respect when others were around that it made the lie of our marriage ridiculous. I needed to find a way to make things better for all of us.

Chapter 9

Keeping Up a Good Front

Our first home had been remodeled, and it was time to draw up plans for the new house we wanted to build on our piece of land. There was no time to take a breath and enjoy what we already had. Dean was determined to have a big house on a nice piece of land. His mother told me that this had always been a dream of his. We had bought two acres in a beautiful location and started planning for the new house. He did a lot of the drawings, and I put the financial information together. I started looking at the financials and researching where to get a construction mortgage.

We had a disagreement one evening, and I decided to leave and take the kids to California to see my family. I made arrangements, called Mom and Dad, and flew home with the kids. Mom and Dad thought it was strange that after all these years that I was finally coming for a visit, especially without Dean. I had not been home since we left there in 1964. I didn't really tell anyone about my problems or that an argument was the reason I'd come back.

After being there a couple of days, I received a dozen roses from Dean. Of course, this softened me up, and I started feeling guilty for leaving—what an emotional roller coaster. My dad told me that I should have had Dean come with me instead of coming alone and missing him so much. Dad wouldn't have thought things were as bad as they were by the way I acted. I tried to enjoy myself with the kids and the family. My sisters Lauren, Lee, and Susan were married and living nearby. Marie and Jerry were still living at home with my parents. My brother Ted had moved away and was in college at the time. My youngest brother, Jerry, was born a couple of months before David. Jerry, Kim, and David were very close in age, so they got along well and had a good time together. It was quite funny that Jerry was their uncle and younger than Kim. The vacation ended with good times to remember, and the three of us went home.

Things returned to normal—whatever that is—and life went on. My job was coming along, the kids were doing well, and we had met a new couple whom Dean worked with. We started bowling with them on a league and got together at our home to visit. Through time, we became aware that they were into the drug scene. They smoked grass and offered us a joint one night. We decided to try it, and it really threw me for a loop. I was scared and had Dean call our friend to make sure that what I was feeling was okay. They just laughed at me and said I would be fine. At that time, grass was pretty popular, and a lot of people our age and younger were using it. It definitely mellowed me out and made life with Dean much more tolerable. Thank heavens it was not an addictive habit for me. Dean tried to get me to try other drugs as he did. I always felt he was trying to get control of me and thought drugs would drag me down. I refused, and he did as he wanted.

Our relationship continued as usual. Based on his mood and my compliance, we were still on the roller coaster. The physical and emotional abuse continued when the spoiled adult threw his tantrums. I guess he was not getting the response he wanted, so he decided to up the game. One evening, Dean took out a hunting knife, put it to my throat, and scared the devil out of me. I backed down and cooperated with his requests. Most of his demands in these situations were related to sex. As you may have already surmised, I did what I had to that evening. You would think that would have scared me enough to leave or do something about it. I would go to work, and people would see marks on my neck. They thought they were hickeys. I just laughed, but inside I was scared and ashamed.

We finally built our home and moved in before it was all finished. We had to sell both of our other houses to pay for the new one. We had a mortgage, but the costs of building far exceeded the mortgage. It was very stressful managing the bills, working, caring for the kids, and especially dealing with my demanding husband.

We had the boat and went out often, but in the winter, we took up snow skiing. It was a good way to have the family together and keep the kids away from friends who were up to no good. Skiing comes naturally to many but not to me. I was afraid of heights and had to learn gradually by going up towropes and eventually the real ski lifts. It took awhile, but the enjoyment that I saw in my kids was well worth it. At times they took their friends, and I saw a lot of happiness in their faces as we went on many weekends together. We enjoyed many times together and great dinners in the evening with the kids and friends.

We rented a house with Dora and Jim and had a good time. Dora did not ski, but she enjoyed getting away and enjoying the beautiful mountains. There were many good times to remember with family and friends. I treasure looking back on the good memories we had together.

I really liked Dora and Jim and looked forward to our times together. I truly believe that the only reason Dean would get together with them is because I worked for Jim. We were invited to a Christmas party at Dora and Jim's home, and I was to bake a cheesecake. I was really looking forward to the party. Dean got into one of his moods, and we got into an argument. He would often do this when we were supposed to go out with friends or do something special. I saw this as a pattern and finally had it with the situation and him. I left and went to Dora and Jim's. I had no family nearby or anywhere to escape to. I went to their house, and they gladly helped me out. They were confused as to why I would leave, so I finally told them the truth. I was there for the party with their friends and made excuses as to why Dean wasn't there. He called me the next day and convinced me to come home. It was just one of the many times I heard him say, "Come home; we will work things out."

I went home, we made up, and life went on. We were always very busy with day-to-day stuff and our jobs. After leaving Dean for the first time, I really started to think about our marriage and the abuse that I had been dealing with over the years. Just telling Jim and Dora the truth about our relationship had taken a lot of stress off of me. I was relieved to have someone else to talk to about my situation. One day, Dean was being his typical obnoxious self and was pushing me around again. I finally got the courage to take a chance and defend myself. I went crazy and started punching him and screaming that he would have to kill me. I fought back and told him if he did kill me, the guys in prison would have a good time with him. He stopped, and for some reason, he never hit me again. However, he was still verbally abusive.

He turned to other things then, like accusing me of having affairs. Looking back, this guy had more problems than I would have ever imagined. It was incredible to me that he turned out to be nothing like what I *thought* he was when I met him. It took courage to fight him, because some women do not get off so easily. Some guys are more violent and determined to hurt them after being confronted. You never know whom you are up against in this situation.

Around 1979, Dean's brother Carl lost his job in Massachusetts. He was married a few years after us and divorced after about ten years. Carl was a great guy. He was very overweight but would give you the shirt off his back. He was crazy about his wife and was very upset when she found someone else through her job. He became bitter about marriage after that. When they were married, Carl and his wife would visit us and bring all kinds of food for me to cook. They didn't cook much, so it was an even swap.

After Carl lost his job, I got his resume and submitted it where I worked. It was a manufacturing facility, and that was his field. He got the job and moved in with us. Carl was very generous and bought many things for all of us. He definitely kept us in food. He was nice to talk to and worked nights, so we didn't see him a lot. Carl wasn't much into housekeeping, so I did find some of his habits difficult. One day, I told Dean that I could not handle cleaning a big house, doing laundry, taking care of him and the kids, and working. So, we got a housekeeper—thank God. She came in once a week, which helped tremendously.

While Carl was with us, my sister Lauren came to visit with her daughter, Danielle. I enjoyed having her around. Carl and Lauren sat up many nights talking. I think he had a crush on her. They remained friends, but that was it. Lauren had gotten a divorce and was trying to obtain skills for employment. I tried to help her improve her typing skills to obtain an office job and eventual a career. She spent many nights learning to type and went home after a couple of months to find a job and build a life for herself and her daughter. I have always had a good relationship with Lauren. She is quiet and one of the best I know at home decorating, sewing, and making beautiful things—that lady can do anything. She has helped decorate my homes many times when I've moved. She is an excellent seamstress, which is not my forte. It is a gift, and she has it.

Carl and Dean were not much alike and did not get along well. They really didn't have a lot in common except for the fact that they were brothers. I put the burden on Dean to talk to his brother about his hygiene. Dean had a real problem dealing with this, and it went on for a long time. I don't think Dean ever talked to him frankly. They just got into a rift over Carl wanting to bring a junk car into the driveway, and he moved out. Carl was with us for about three years, and I did feel bad that he had to move out.

Carl moved out in 1982, and around the same time, my father-in-law was laid off from his job. He needed to find a job.

Oh my—I was not looking forward to this one. I got his resume and saw an ad in the local newspaper looking for his expertise in manufacturing. I thought of ignoring it, because I knew that it would lead to him moving in with us. But, I knew that I had to call him; he ending up getting an interview and the job. He moved in with us, while Dean's mom was still working in Massachusetts. She was very upset about having to quit her job and move, but there were no other alternatives. Dean's dad and I got along well. By that time, I'd taken up drinking wine, so we used to sit, talk, and drink wine—we got along fine.

About six months later, my mother-in-law quit her job, sold their house, and prepared to move in with us. I had a good job that required a lot of my time, seven days a week. The kids had a lot going on, Dean was demanding, my father-in-law lived with us, and now my mother-in-law was coming to live with us. I think I was ready for a nervous breakdown. I had to stay cool.

I contacted a realtor friend and told her that my in-laws were looking for a home. She found a duplex that was close to us and reasonable. They loved the house and got a good deal. My mother-in-law was only with us for a few weeks. I liked her, but she was very opinionated and quite negative. I don't deal well with people who have negative attitudes. I like the optimist and need that in my life.

Everyone had moved into their own homes, and things were back to some kind of normal—at least normal for us. As long as Dean and I had to concentrate on others, we didn't get into it as much. He also had to put on a good show while his parents lived with us. Now that everyone was gone, we had to focus on our relationship again.

I will say that I personally believe that Dean was a sex addict. He had to have sex most days, which was exhausting for me. Sex is not much fun when you feel like you have to do it and there's no real intimacy involved. He never understood that. I think sometimes I equate sex with affection. I may not be a very affectionate person because of this and other things in my life. After so many years, I adjusted and thought the alternative was more difficult than putting up with the sex. That's not a good thing, but I dealt with it at the time.

Kim graduated from a Catholic high school in 1981 and moved to a state college about two hours away from home. We bought her a small car so she could go back and forth. She had to live off campus with three other girls who were juniors and seniors. By the time she decided which college to attend, all on-campus housing was filled up. Her living situation wasn't good. They partied too much, and she had terrible grades. She brought friends home on weekends, and we had many good times; however, her grades declined because of her partying.

After the first year, she came home for the summer, and I told her that I was not paying for partying and lousy grades. She got a job for the summer and took a semester off. She moved back home, worked at a fast food place, and dated a few guys.

Kim had dated a guy in high school whom she was crazy about. His name was Tom, and she'd met him on a class trip. They had many good times together, but his family was not too keen on their dating. Kim ended up in the hospital for some surgery while in high school, and Tom ended up breaking up with her. I don't know why or what the real issue was, but Kim was devastated when this happened. It wasn't a good time, but eventually, she dealt with it. She always had a crush on Tom through high school and even when he went away to college.

Kim dated while she was home. She had a crazy-looking guy show up at the door, but we welcomed him and hoped she would not get involved. I always hoped she would get back with Tom, because I really liked him and thought he would be very successful in life. Tom left for college, and they both went their separate ways. Kim returned to college, and it was close enough for her to live at home. She was doing well, and things were looking up.

Chapter 10

My Life Changed Forever

In 1980, I started a new job with a government contractor as a systems programmer and worked my way into management. I thoroughly enjoyed my work and was well respected by the people I worked for and with. My job was one that required my presence seven days a week, but I always figured that the better I did my job the fewer phone calls I would receive. I often had to go into work in the middle of the night or spend twenty-four-hour stints fixing problems. The job was a real challenge but well worth it. My salary more than took care of our household expenses, and we were able to travel a bit on the company. Times were good, and I felt everything was getting better.

Things were going well, and the company I worked for was in the middle of a major system conversion that took many long hours and a lot of planning for things to be implemented well. I had gotten home from work and got a call that my son had been in a dirt-bike accident. It was three days before his eighteenth birthday, and the police called and asked Dean and I to come to the hospital. The police had gone through an emergency service operator to contact us. We had an unlisted phone number, and on the way to the hospital, I thought about that. Why did David not give them our phone number? The more I thought about this, the more worried I became.

I knew something was really wrong when we entered the hospital. Too many people were concerned, and they took us into a separate room. My son had borrowed a friend's dirt bike to go to the corner store, and as he rounded a turn, he hit a curb. He had no helmet on, and the back of his head hit the only rock on the road. He was immediately unconscious and was in a coma. A lady in the neighborhood had seen the accident and tried to help him. He ended up having a brain stem injury, and the neurologist told us he would not be the same person upon waking up. They had no idea how long it would take or what the results would be.

David was in intensive care, and I prayed day and night that he would survive. I remember thinking that I didn't care what his disabilities might be; I just wanted him to live. We could only see him three times a day for an hour each time while he was in intensive care. I would get up in the middle of the night and call the nurses to find out if he was okay. It was scary talking to David and having absolutely no response.

The brain stem controls many bodily functions, including temperature. He had to be put on what I would call ice to keep his body temperature down. He broke out in a terrible skin problem, but I don't know what caused that. All I know is that he was lying there in a bed and not responding to anyone or anything.

I went to work after the first week and then traveled back and forth to the hospital. The people who worked for me were very supportive and took over the planned conversion. I did the best I could to be engaged, but my primary concern was David. Dean and I would just sit and talk to him about everything that was happening on a day-to-day basis, hoping he could hear us and it would help. Just in case he heard us, we did not talk about his health or his situation. No negative conversation was allowed. It was exhausting.

Kim's boyfriend at the time, Dale, stayed at the house with us after David's accident. David's girlfriend also stayed with us. Kim was annoyed because I gave so much attention to David's girlfriend. But for me, she was a part of David that I could still relate to. Time went on, and after about five weeks, he came out of the coma. The doctor was right; he did not wake up and say,

"Hi, Mom." He could not talk, walk, or breathe on his own, and he acted panicky. He'd lost a lot of weight and by that time was being fed by a tube in his stomach. Friends from school would come to see him, and I saw the shock in their faces when they saw him. It was tough for everyone. He pushed people away. One day while Kim was feeding him, he bit her. The hospital said this was all normal for a person with a head injury; an anger phase was common, and it was also possible that he was somehow trying to communicate. After all, he could not talk.

Once the doctors realized his general health was okay, he had to be moved to a hospital for rehabilitation. David was moved by ambulance to a rehabilitation center about an hour away from home. There were many other kids his age in the facility with all kinds of different injuries, mostly from automobile crashes. A number of them had brain stem injuries like David. David had to learn to walk and talk all over again. He was a difficult patient and had to be tied to the bed, because he kept trying to get out. He used a board to spell out things. They gave him occupational, physical, and speech therapy for months.

Each day that we visited there, it was helpful to talk to other parents in similar situations. There was one boy named John who couldn't talk or communicate. He just looked at you, and I could tell he understood me when I talked to him. You can see it in their eyes. A brain stem injury has a slow recovery process, and some never function normally again. I never met his family and felt very badly for him and others. A young girl had turned eighteen and been given a new car. She let her boyfriend drive, and he slammed into a tree. She was still in a coma, and I would visit her. Her parents were devastated. I tried to encourage them because of slow improvements with David. I saw the girl's tears run down the side of her face, but that is all she could do. I felt so sad and helpless seeing what such devastating injuries do to families and the children. The hospital only keeps them so long, and then they have to go to a long-term care facility. After meeting some of these people, I thought we were lucky.

The social worker at both hospitals recommended that we get some counseling as a family. Dean was not interested at all. He was already perfect, remember? I participated in a group and found it to be very helpful. Dean and I went back and forth to the rehab hospital about three times a week. It was very difficult, because we had full time jobs. After about three months, David came home. This was good; we could be around him more often and could stop the running back and forth. Dean and I were doing all right, because we had our son to concentrate on.

When he came home, David could barely stand up alone. Kim was home, and we had to depend on her to help David. She was resentful of the attention David had been getting, so she was not too cooperative in helping him. I had a hard time dealing with this. I could not understand why his sister was not more supportive. I began to think she had become a very selfish individual.

David could hardly get around on his own, and his voice was barely audible. He was still very impulsive, and his IQ testing was very low. His fine motor skills were terrible, so he had a hard time trying to use eating utensils, which made it difficult for him to eat or drink. He was very dependent on others; this had to have been very difficult for him to accept. He had quite a head injury, and some of his disabilities would remain for life. It is a shame when we deal with people who have disabilities and we cannot be more supportive. People often don't understand unless it is them that it happens to. Some are very small minded.

At the time, the doctors could not tell what would be permanent or temporary. In these situations, medical professionals simply say they don't know. We just have to wait and see.

During the next six months, we tried to help David and got him back into his last year of high school. He went back in a wheelchair and was in a special program. His girlfriend stopped coming around, and they no longer communicated. The school had to provide transportation, as well as physical and occupational therapy. They were responsible for David's education until he graduated from high school or turned twenty-one. They allowed him to graduate that year, although I definitely did not think he was at a level to pass his classes. It was more of a one-on-one class structure. The system will push through many kids to avoid costly responsibilities.

After David's accident, my life changed forever, and my attitude did as well. I became less tolerant of Dean's crap and of him in general. I started drinking more wine, which made me more vocal in our arguments. It is said that sometimes drinking makes you braver. It is so in my case. I started to say exactly what I thought about Dean and about everything else. He then started accusing me of fooling around with our friend Jim and Dean's younger brother Joe. I thought he was nuts and was defending myself all the time. I left him a few times and stayed with two different women whom I had worked with at other companies.

In the past, I had gone to Jim and Dora's, but I did not want to keep getting them involved all the time. I often felt bad that I would go there so upset and then go home. I am sure it was very frustrating for them as well. One of the women I had worked with told me she thought I really needed some counseling. I guess it wouldn't take a rocket scientist to figure that out. I knew Dean would never go, but I needed to talk to someone.

Kim had broken up with Dale and had started seeing Tom again. This was good, and she was happy about it. She was in college and pursuing her future with Tom. She lacked patience with David and complained about his actions. I guess this would be expected, but I do believe she was a bit insensitive to her brother's situation. Family counseling was out, but I could help myself.

I contacted the counselor recommended by my friend. He was a bit different than what I had expected. Bucky came to my house and looked like a lumberjack, casually dressed in shorts and a beard. When I first saw him, I wondered how I would ever be able to talk to him. Dean went upstairs while we talked and let me know he did not approve of the counseling. I think sometimes he listened to what I was saying.

I liked Bucky and wanted to start seeing him on a regular basis. Dean would not have this and would give me a hard time until I cancelled my appointments. Bucky went back and forth with me and my appointments. He knew what was happening and why. A couple of times while I was talking with Bucky, Dean would come downstairs. He would start yelling, pounding on the glass table, and arguing with Bucky about how wrong I was and how hard it was to live with me. Bucky tried everything to get Dean involved with counseling. I felt like Bucky turned on me a few times and sided with Dean to get him involved, but nothing worked. After Dean got it out of his system, he would go back upstairs and refuse to participate. There was nothing wrong with him; it was always me. That was okay, though. I continued to see Bucky on a regular basis to help myself. We can't force others to do anything.

After David was able to walk and get around on his own, we sent him to my parents' home in California for a couple of weeks. My sister Marie helped him a lot and was trying to teach him to swim. He just sunk in the pool, which surprised him since he'd been able to swim before. When he left California, he went to my aunt Rosemary's in Michigan for a week or so. She had six kids, and they were all great for David. As I remember back, I think about how it must have been hard for her family to deal with David's situation. He was barely able to get around and could not communicate well at all. His cousins knew the old David but not the new one. She had great kids, and they were very supportive of each other. David's time away gave us a bit of a break to hopefully get our act together.

After David returned home, we decided to take the kids and drive to my aunt Rosemary's in Michigan for Thanksgiving. A lot of my brothers and sisters, my parents, and many other relatives were there for the holiday. My sister Lee was there and had gotten divorced. Dean decided to play a little game with me and followed her all around the house, flirting and carrying on. He looked so ridiculous. After what had happened at our home before with Lee and Dean, I was pissed to say the least. My aunt and mom saw the crap and were upset as well. It was a very embarrassing and stressful time spent with the family.

On the way home, Dean and I didn't talk at all. I am sure that made the kids very uncomfortable, because the trip took about eight hours. When I got home, I called my sister Marie and asked if she wanted to find an apartment with me. I'd had it with Dean's games and was resolved to end the marriage. I just couldn't believe how far he would go to upset me and believed he really didn't care that much about what I thought at all.

My job was moving along, and I had been promoted to supervise a group of programmers. This meant a lot more responsibility and off-hours work, but I loved the job. I always felt that I wasn't the same person at work that I was at home. I asked Bucky why I felt so much different between work and home. He told me that I should be able to feel and act the same at home as work. That definitely sounded foreign to me.

People whom I worked for and with supported me very well through tough times with David, but they knew nothing about my personal relationship problems. I was very good at hiding things from people. I couldn't have anyone know how miserable I truly was or what a mess I had for a husband. People at work respected me, and I couldn't lay out all of my problems at home; they might not think so well of me if I did. Besides, it was all so negative and convoluted. I needed a place where existence was positive and that gave me the emotional strength I didn't find at home.

Through all my years of marriage to Dean, I was threatened with divorce. We finally came to a point when we were seriously discussing divorce. It almost felt like it was a game of chicken with him. We put together a divorce agreement that could be agreed to by both of us. I felt like I was getting a raw deal; my victim mentality at the time didn't help the situation. I moved out again, stayed with a lady near work, and rented a room from her. I was always the one who had to move out. He wasn't going anywhere. David was able to get around on his own fairly well by this time and stayed in the house with his father. I continued to pay the bills, including the housekeeper and my own room rent. Of course, he called. After about four weeks, I moved back home. We had a big picnic, and everyone came over for the party.

Yes, hope must spring eternally.

Chapter 11

Pray for the Strength to Do What Is Right

I moved in and out a lot and kept seeing my counselor. When Dean would become verbally abusive or accuse me of running around, I would become fed up and leave. This was really tough on the kids even though they were older. They didn't understand, and I couldn't help them out. Of course, Dean would use David as an excuse for why I was leaving, which was sick. I found it very difficult to leave my son with his dad, but it was better than staying and having him listen to all the arguing. I knew that eventually it would work out for all of us.

For years, Dean had been accusing me of having affairs with his brother Joe and our friend Jim. He was so desperate that he called one day from work and asked me if I had an affair with Joe or Jim. I said no and went on with my day. Little did I know that he recorded my answers and took a tape to a no-name voice stress analysis guy.

The guy told him I was lying, and Dean came home and confronted me. I was furious and went with him to see this guy. I retook the test (stupid me), and once again, the guy said I was lying. Only this time he said I was lying about one man but not the other. I forget who was who. That is about how credible these guys are. After that, Dean was convinced he was right—what a jerk.

Bucky had a fit that I would do such a stupid thing by going to take this test. I realized that after the fact, but oh well.

Dean kept accusing and questioning. We went back and forth and eventually agreed to sign a divorce agreement distributing everything among us. We signed our divorce papers on Valentine's Day 1985, and then we both went home. Dean filed for divorce, but we still lived together. The notice would come for us to go to court, and if we were getting along, we did not go. He called off the divorce (must have had a good day), but the same roller coaster continued.

Little did I know that in those days, the person who filed was the only one who had to show up in court or call it off. I finally filed for divorce. This was probably a good thing for me. When I was notified of the court date, we argued all night. I told him that if he did not say he believed me about the so-called affairs, I would go to court and get the divorce. I was so upset and tired of the accusations and the deceit; I just wanted it to end. It was so upsetting to me that he would not believe me, and I finally understood that our marriage was going to come to an end.

We both went to court the next day and got a divorce in August 1985. The judge seemed to agree that the agreement we made was fair, and we were divorced. We then both went home and lived together. I know this sounds like a very strange arrangement to most people. I felt relieved that divorce was not being held over my head, and I was free to do as I pleased. Plus, I knew separating the financial responsibilities would not be easy. It was going to be tough paying all these bills. I agreed to a 60/40 split, and I paid all my own living expenses and 60 percent of his. Dean had a good job and made decent money at the time. He complained all the time about working for anyone and wanted to be out on his own. Doing what, I don't know. The judge thought our financial split was a fair deal. He was a chauvinistic jerk as well.

Chapter 12

Life after the Divorce

By October, Kim told me that she was pregnant, and she and Tom were going to get married in December. Only a couple of people knew that Dean and I had divorced, so we went on like nothing had happened. The wedding invitations and announcement were by Dean and April, not Mr. and Mrs. Richards. To many, it was confusing, but that was my life.

I had been losing a lot of weight, and the doctor diagnosed me with colitis. He made me take a mild sedative until all the scheduled events were over. It helped a lot. Tom's family was upset about the circumstances but cooperative regarding the quick wedding arrangements. Around the end of November Kim had a miscarriage, but the two of them decided to get married in December as planned.

All of my family came from out of state for Christmas and the wedding. Our house was full of family and fun. Dean and I were getting along well. I told my parents before they came that we had divorced. They didn't understand the situation but accepted it. By the time of the wedding, most of my relatives knew we were not married any longer. Some of our friends knew; others didn't. Everything else was perfect—the wedding was beautiful, and a good time was had by all. Kim and Tom went on their honeymoon and came back before all the family left to go home. My family stayed for New Year's Day and then went home. Things then went back to normal.

By this time, my career was moving along. I transferred within the corporation to be in charge of the information services department. I loved the job, but Dean worked in the same company in the manufacturing department. He would come upstairs to visit, and if I was in a meeting with my boss and the door was closed, it annoyed him. What an insecure guy. His behavior reminded me of years earlier. How funny that we worked for the same company in different positions, but things had not changed. People have meetings with their bosses or departments within closed doors, and it's not a problem to most. How pathetic—his mindset was screwy and more personal than business. He was just too jealous.

Dealing with this was very difficult, and things finally blew up. In November, I moved into a condo with my sister Marie. It was a nice place, but it was difficult for me because I really felt like things were ending. Tom and Kim were celebrating their first Christmas married, and she was expecting Gary in February. It was Christmas and a tough time to be away from the kids. Dean always used the kids as a ploy to keep us together. I always did the Christmas shopping and planning for the holidays. I continued to do this, because I wanted the kids to have a nice Christmas even though we were not together. Kim and David were in there twenties by this time. I bought and wrapped presents for the kids that Dean and I had agreed on; we kept some at his house and the rest at mine. Dean had Christmas Eve with Kim, Tom, and David, and then they came to see me.

Marie and I had a scraggly tree, and I was lost without the kids for the holiday. They ended up coming for an hour or so late on Christmas Eve and planned to leave the next day for New Hampshire with their father. They dropped the dog off to stay with me. I'd had the dog for several years, but Dean would not let me take her when I left. Can you imagine how he would have been about the kids? I took care of the dog, and Marie and I did the best we could for the rest of the holiday. I do know it was kind of lonely for both of us.

Marie and I made a last-minute decision to head to Michigan for New Year's Eve. We both had that week off, and our aunt Rosemary loved to have us visit. It was a great time for us. Marie did most of the driving. I was not as confident when it came to road trips. I never had to drive as long as Dean was with me.

We had a great time, and I am glad we went to spend this time with Aunt Rosemarie. It was a memorable time for all of us. Marie and I made it home safely and went back to work for the New Year. Dean started calling after the holidays, but I didn't respond well. I was seeing Bucky on a regular basis and was trying to be strong and stay away.

I was starting a new life and decided to go to college. My boss told me that with all the experience I had in information services, I should not worry about getting a degree. He felt that I had enough experience and a degree was not necessary. I felt that not having a degree may be a reason in the future for another company to hold me back from moving up in my job.

It was tough going to school in the evening after working all day, but I wanted to do it. I decided to get a bachelor of science in psychology. I had moved into management positions, and knowing more about people would be a bigger benefit. I was starting to get away from most of the day-to-day technical skills. My first semester was in 1987. Kim had already graduated from college and had a good job as an applications programmer. I had gotten her interviews where I worked, and she landed a job. They said she was a very good programmer and had a good future in the field.

Dean kept calling, and in February, I agreed to go on a ski trip with him for a weekend. We had a good time, but I fell and ended up in a cast for six weeks. Marie helped me a lot dealing with that cast. She helped me in the shower, washed my hair, and dealt with a tough time. Fortunately, it was my left arm, so I could still work and do some things.

I am sure Marie was a bit disappointed that I had started to see Dean again. She helped me so much, and I did not want to start dealing with starting my life over. Instead, I would go and spend the weekends with Dean but not move back. He was so nice to me and very charming. He gave me a lot of attention, and we went on a couple of very nice vacations together. On my fortieth birthday, he gave me forty beautiful roses, my favorite flower. We then went on a vacation to the Caribbean. We were discussing getting remarried and moving back in together when we decided to go to Florida for a week.

I knew that I had to pay a penalty for getting out of my lease and talked to Marie about what she would do if I moved back home. She had a friend whom she could move in with and was very patient and cooperative with me in this situation. I don't know if in the same situation, I would have been as understanding.

While we were in Florida, signs of the same old Dean came back. He became demanding, and I rebelled. I remember leaving our bedroom and going to another room and staring out the window; I knew that things had not changed. It was sad, but I finally learned after twenty-four years that leopards never change their spots. I only use this terminology because one of my bosses told me that when I got divorced. Dean and I returned, and I decided not to move back at this time. I guess I always hoped something magical would happen, and we could work things out. Maybe I was always a dreamer.

We returned home from Florida and were sitting on the balcony outside our bedroom when I told him that I was not moving back. He was upset and playing his silent game. I stayed over that night and slept on the couch downstairs.

In the middle of the night, I felt someone tugging at me. I awoke and said, "What do you want?"

It was Dean, and he was on his knees saying his chest hurt. I was going to call 911, but he told me not to. He went upstairs, and I followed. He felt a pain in his jaw and agreed to have me take him to the hospital. I drove, and when we arrived at the hospital, he did not want me to drop him off at the door. He wanted to park and walk—what a bunch of macho bullshit. When we went in, I told the nurses the problem, and they immediately put him in a wheelchair. He was very lucky, because he'd had a heart attack and a vessel opened up at the same time so he didn't have any heart damage. He went into intensive care.

I let his family know what had happened and went back to our house with the kids. Dean's parents and his brother Joe came over to the house. Joe was going to go to the hospital to see his brother. I had been told by the doctors that no one should visit him who could upset him. I pretty much stayed away, because every time I went in, the heart monitor beeped because he would get upset.

I finally told Dean's parents and Joe that Dean had been accusing me of having an affair with Joe. I told Joe he could not go see his brother. He was very upset and thought it was a stupid thing that Dean had been thinking. It was a relief to finally be honest with them about Dean's bizarre thinking. That ended Joe and Dean's relationship for good. I honestly believe that Dean was jealous of Joe's relationship with his parents and wanted to put a wedge between them.

Sibling rivalry can be strange, and Dean was always Mama's little boy, even though Joe was the youngest. It is a shame, but it isn't my problem anymore. To this day, I continue to keep in touch with Joe and his wife. He says his brother is a toxic person, and he stays away from him. I do have to agree with that. It is so sad that one person can cause so many problems within a family. Dean caused many people in his family to divide and not talk to each other. His parents were caught up in this, and I do know they were very upset with him and the situation.

I had agreed to move back to our home before going to Florida, and when Dean had his heart attack, I felt that I needed to move back home and take care of him. I had given up the condo before we went away, and Marie moved me back home while I worked and visited Dean at the hospital. Marie was so supportive in my situation—much more than many sisters would ever be. I was told to not upset Dean, so I bit my tongue. I knew that our being together was not going to happen and prepared to eventually leave for good. After a couple of weeks, Dean came home from the hospital. The doctor gave him sedatives to take that made him sleep a lot. He was out of work for a few months and went to physical therapy. We didn't have much of a relationship, and I kept a low profile as to not argue. Of course, he accused me of being the reason that he had his heart attack. I ignored the remarks and went on with my life. David was at home, and Kim and Tom were living in their own home. Kim was pregnant and expecting in February.

Dean went back to work in September, and I knew that I would move out soon. When I had previously moved to the condo with Marie, Dean gave me a hard time and blamed Marie for my moving out. I told him she had nothing to do with it. He believed whatever his crazy mind wanted to. I told him I was going to find an apartment by myself and move out. He said okay and helped me move into a studio apartment in October 1987.

As usual, I wasn't in the apartment for more than a few days before he called me. I told him it was over, but he persisted. Bucky was coming over to see me, and Dean knew he would be there. Dean showed up at the door and came upstairs. He acknowledged Bucky and said to him, "See what she is doing again?"

I told Dean to leave and explained that it was over. I had to tell him this a few times before he left. Bucky gave me a hug and said, "Finally, you did it. I am so proud of you."

That was the last time I saw Bucky. I talked to him a few times over the phone, but I knew what I had to do.

Chapter 13

My New Life Starts

It was tough living alone and being without the kids. I worked a lot and was taking at least three classes at night. I had to start at the bottom in college and found it to be a real challenge. It is not easy to start college when you are forty years old. I attended at night, but there were a lot of kids in my class who were younger than my own children. Plus, working a full-time job and going to school in the evening can be exhausting. David was with his dad, and Kim was with Tom. I knew I had to rebuild my life and found a women's support group to help me with that transition.

I met some women with similar situations, and we had great conversation. I had seen an ad for a church singles' group that met nearby. I was hesitant to go because I knew nothing about them. At one of the women's support group meetings, I asked the counselor if that particular singles' group was okay and a safe place to join. She assured me it was a good group, and I decided to go to one of their meetings.

There must have been 150 people at the meeting when I walked in alone. They gave me a name tag so people knew that I was new to the group. Actually, I think the single guys wanted to know who was new. It was kind of weird. They broke people up into groups and had a topic for the night. I knew I was screwed up, but some of them were much worse. Hard to believe, huh? I went a couple of times, and after one meeting, the group stopped at a club close by that had a band. I went with them, and that was the night I met Matt. Matt was a nice-looking guy and ten years younger than me. He asked me to dance, and the next thing you know, we were dating.

In the meantime, Dean kept calling me. I guess he thought, as usual, that I was coming back. I knew that if I was involved with anyone else, he would be convinced that I was not coming back. Matt and I got into a relationship quickly, and he started staying over. I had him answer the phone one night when Dean called, and that ended the phone calls.

Dean was still staying at the house, and I would go over to the house once a month to go through the bills and make sure everything was being paid. The last time I went over there, he tried to kiss me and I pulled away. I was involved with Matt and was not playing his game. Dean has hated me from that day forward. Matt didn't understand why I had to go over there to pay bills, and he was right. I had enabled Dean way too long.

I was responsible for paying 60 percent of our expenses and told Dean that he had to pay certain bills on his own. Of course, I had to give him money to ensure everything was paid. He had his house, Corvette, boat, and housekeeper and was living the single life. I didn't care. I just wanted the house to sell so we could get on with our lives.

Kim had Gary in February 1988, and she and Tom were very happy. She went back to work, and I looked forward to spending time with my grandson. Matt and I were traveling a bit, and we went to New York City frequently. We went to a few plays (my first time to a play in New York City). We went to China Town, Little Italy, and a number of other places. I was enjoying my single life and moved into a larger condo. Work was going very well.

David was able to get around fairly well and was even able to drive a car. We had a drivers education group evaluate him, and they said he could drive. I was not comfortable with this, but he started to drive and get around on his own. It had been about five years since his accident, and he needed to get a job. His balance and coordination was not good, but he interviewed for a job in manufacturing where I worked and started by moving parts around the factory. I also managed to get Tom and Marie interviews at the company, and they were both hired. Unfortunately, the whole family was dependent on the same corporation. David moved in with me because I lived close to work. He brought the dog with him. She was getting older and having problems by this time.

The people David worked for and with were very patient with him at work, because they knew he had a severe disability. He complained about the job but did not realize how lucky he was to have one. A guy who worked for me was a good friend of Dean and hung around with him a lot, especially in the summer because they would go out on the boat. I often heard them talking (probably so I would hear) about the fun they had on the weekend and the young girls whom Dean was hanging out with. I ignored them and considered the source. I never let my personal relationships affect my job or managing the department. This same guy mentioned to me one day that he had to go over to my house and put out pans to collect the water that was coming through the roof when it rained. I was shocked because the house was only twenty years old. I knew there was no point in talking to Dean, because I had offered to buy the house at one time, and he definitely would not do it. He had also been laid off from the company. He didn't seem to be worried and spent a lot of time having a good time. He always disliked working for anyone.

I contacted a lawyer and had to file against him because he wasn't meeting the divorce agreement criteria. It cost me $1,500 for a lawyer, and we met about the roof. My lawyer said he was letting the house fall apart and wasn't even looking for work. We agreed that I would buy the shingles, and he and his friends would fix the roof. Oh well, it cost me money, but the house would be in better shape. The house was not selling because of these problems plus the decorations and colors were dated to the seventies.

In the meantime, Matt and I were living together, and I had met his family. They were very nice people, and we spent a lot of time with them. I think they had reservations because I was forty and he was thirty. They also knew I was a young grandmother, and I think that was weird for his mother.

Gary was getting bigger, and Kim shared time seeing her father and me. I was enjoying being a grandmother, and before long, Kim was pregnant again with Alexandra.

One day I began to think about Dean's financial situation. Being out of work and partying, was he paying his bills? I would give him a check, and he was supposed to pay the bills and mortgage with the money. I decided to call the mortgage company and found out that he was three months behind on the payments. I was shocked but not entirely surprised. I always took care of the finances when we were together and took pride in paying bills on time. I knew there would be no sense in talking to Dean. The kids told me they could not even mention my name, and he called me every name in the book—even in front of my kids and grandkids. They just avoided mentioning anything about me. It was no use trying to have them talk any sense into him. I think that was his way of manipulating them.

I called a woman at the mortgage company and told her I had the money to pay the bills but would only do so if he sold me the house. I told her that she better call him and scare the crap out of him, or I would let the house go. She did call and got him to move. I gave him twenty thousand dollars and took over all the bills. He moved out and went south.

I moved back into the house in 1990. It was outdated and needed a lot of work. There were a lot of memories for me there, and I was not looking forward to any of the memories or the work to change the house into my home. It had been my home for years; some memories were good, but others were not. The house had deteriorated through the years, and there was a lot of work to be done plus a big investment of cash. David was with me, and eventually, Kim, Tom, and Gary moved in too. Kim had to quit her job as a programmer when she was pregnant with Alexandra. She was traveling a long way to get to work, and it was taking a toll on her. They could not afford their home without her working, so they sold it and moved in with me. It worked out for all of us. I started remodeling the house by having all the carpeting removed and updating the décor. This also helped me feel better about living there.

Matt and I began to drift apart. We had been together for three years. We went to a Christmas party where he worked, and he ended up getting drunk and punching his boss—not a good thing to do. While I was trying to get him to leave, he pushed me; that was enough for me. His father had a temper, and I already learned this stuff can run in families. One Sunday morning in January, I woke up and told him that it was over. We parted ways, and the relationship ended. There were no hard feelings either way.

My work and school kept me busy. Kim, Tom, Gary, Alexandra, and David all lived with me. Tom was working and in law school. Kim was at home and taking premed classes in the evening. They had decided that after Tom graduated from law school and took the bar exam, she would go to medical school. She had a degree in computer science and programming experience, but that wasn't enough for her. She felt if Tom could have his dream of law school, she could have hers of being a doctor.

I always felt that I worked a lot in my career and missed out on much of my life with my kids. Dean took too much of my attention as well. I warned Kim about the ramifications of starting another career with such small babies, but she did as she wanted. Maybe this runs in the family.

I returned to the church singles' group meetings, and many friends who were there three years earlier were still attending. A group of women and I went to various dances and had a good time together. We went to New York City a couple of times to various clubs, and it was a lot of fun.

I also joined a company that matched you up with other people. I thought it was an opportunity to meet someone my own age and with a good profession. They matched me up with a few people whom I could not relate to at all. They were all very successful but seemed a bit chauvinistic to me. I ran quickly from that kind of guy. One guy was interesting, and I dated him a few times, but we didn't click. I had learned in the women's group that I was attracted to a certain type of person who may not be good for me. I realized that I was attracted to what I call a "macho bullshit" kind of guy. Recognizing that was so good for me. People often don't give other types of personalities a chance when they are dating. I learned to step back and look at the person.

The church group had dances at the Holiday Inn on Sundays. I decided to go with a friend and met Richard that night. We had a good time, and my friend asked on our way home if I liked him. I told her he was a nice guy and I might go out with him, but nothing else would come of it. Richard did call me, and we started dating once a week. He would call midweek and ask me out for Saturday night. This was fine by me because I was dating a guy who wanted to go out during the middle of the week. Richard and I met at places the first few times. I didn't want him to know where I lived, and I was more comfortable taking my own car.

Our first real date was meeting for dinner at seven o'clock in the evening, and we didn't leave the restaurant until closing. We just sat and talked. It was great conversation, and I was beginning to really like him. How refreshing to be able to have an intelligent conversation! On my birthday, I invited Richard over, and the guy I had been dating in the middle of the week called. I suddenly felt that I needed to be honest with both of these guys. That evening I told Richard I had been dating someone else during the week. He wasn't concerned about that. I was surprised. The next evening, I told the other guy the same thing, and he was fine with it too. Well, I wasn't comfortable with the situation and knew that Richard was the person for me. I quit seeing the other guy.

Richard had lost his job as an industrial engineer and was living in a very nice condo. We dated for a few months and then became involved. He became the love of my life, and we could really relate on just about everything.

I told my daughter and Marie that I would marry him someday. I think they were surprised. Because I knew his situation, I asked him to rent out his condo and move in with us. I told my daughter that he was moving in, and she had an absolute fit. I thought, *Wow, whose house is this anyway and who is paying the bills?* I ignored her, and Richard moved in with us.

The house was huge, and Kim, Tom, and the kids had really taken over most of it. Until Richard pointed it out, I didn't realize that they used the whole house, and I stayed in my room most of the time. I guess going to school and working kept me too busy to notice.

I would clean the house on weekends or hire someone to do it, because my daughter was very sloppy. Richard pointed out that they piled the dishes in the sink and left them there for me. He was right. With so many people living in the house, we had to set up rules. I explained the following to my daughter: "I am home on the weekend, and Kim, you are here all day. Do your laundry during the week. Don't leave dishes in the sink. Pick up after yourself."

Richard was looking for a job and helping at the house. He did a lot of work in the yard and tried to keep out of Kim's way. Eventually, he told me that she talked on the phone all day, ignored the kids, and ran around and picked things up just before I would get home. Over time, I began to realize this was true. She also had a real attitude toward Richard and me. I think her father's way of manipulating passed on to her—make me miserable, and I will give in. That wasn't going to work anymore. Tom was in the middle of everything and tried his best to stay out of it. Richard and Tom did a lot of work on the house, replacing floors and making everything better. I enjoyed having the grandkids around, and Richard was not used to children but dealt with it well.

I finally decided that we needed some peace and quiet. Kim's attitude toward Richard created a stressful environment for all of us. I finally told Kim and Tom that they had to find an apartment of their own. I gave them one year to do this. Kim had a fit, and the next year was difficult to say the least. She was very spoiled and used to getting what she wanted. If she didn't, she would raise cane until you gave in. She did this with Tom and the kids—like father, like daughter.

Richard always tried to approach issues about my kids very carefully. He would try to point out the negative things they were doing and ask me to just be more aware and watch on my own. We never argued about them, because he was very careful about the subject as not to upset me. Kim and Tom found an apartment before the year ended and moved out. She resented it, but it had to be done.

The month Kim and Tom moved out, I found out that my job was being eliminated. I was devastated and just cried for a long time. David had been laid off about six months earlier, and the company was going through a rough time. I was the highest labor grade woman in the company, and my boss had retired. They brought in a hatchet man and did a job on me. This was in May 1992. I was determined to take this time to finish my degree and look for a job. Richard was working as an accountant and rebuilding his career; he helped me through a tough time in my life.

Issues started with David. He would go out at night, and I never knew when he was coming home. I constantly worried about him getting hurt and lost much sleep over this. I had big responsibilities and needed to be able to get some rest. He would come home and tell me about going out with hookers and how one pulled a knife on him. Richard was furious. He said David should never come home and tell me about the horrible things he was doing—that was no way to talk to your mom. I had to agree. The police brought David home one night, because they found him sleeping on the side of the road. I was so embarrassed; we lived in an affluent neighborhood, and here my son was living like a bum.

Richard and I finally told David that he had to be home between eleven o'clock at night and six o'clock in the morning so that I did not have to worry about him and where he was. David immediately decided to do as he pleased, and there was an argument between him and Richard. This upset me, and I decided to make a decision—I told David he had to leave.

He took some of his belongings and had to find a place to live on his own. This was one of the toughest things I did in my life. I found out that David went to the local shelter. I talked to a woman in the social services system about David and his problems. She tried to help him in the system, and he was not aware of my involvement. I needed to know that he was okay and where he was staying. It was just like when I didn't know what my mother was doing to help me when I was a teenager.

I was devastated and was constantly trying to find out where David was and if he was safe. Richard, Kim, Tom, Gary, Alexandra, and I all went down to the local beach to watch the Fourth of July fireworks. David was there and sat with us to watch the fireworks. After they were over, we all left and said good-bye. I knew that David would probably be sleeping on a park bench that night down by the train station. It was heartbreaking for me to leave him that night and walk away. I knew I had to do it and prayed that I was doing the right thing for him.

David went from shelter to shelter, and the woman I had found in social services let me know where he was and applied for disability for him. He was dealing with a traumatic brain injury, and eventually, they found him to be bipolar as well. That is why he would stay in his room for days and sleep or leave the house and be gone all night. A doctor prescribed medication to help him, he was assigned a counselor, and they found various places for him to stay until something else came up that would be more permanent. Over time, I would go over and pick David up and bring him to the house for dinner on the weekend. I would always take him back to where he was staying, because I was afraid to let him stay with us again. We had all been through too much, and he was finally learning to be on his own and be more independent. His counselor was a great guy and tried so hard to help David in the system and financially managed his bills.

David was on disability and had some funds. He could not manage his money at all. The accident had a big impact on his ability to manage money. He spent it on a lot of nonsense and would even give it away to others who were in the places he was living. Through time a friend of Kim's wanted to rent her condo out, and David moved into a place of his own. He rented this condo for a few years, and eventually, he bought the condo with our help with a down payment. He was out on his own, and that was good for him. We gave him some furniture and had him over for dinner occasionally. I finally knew that he could survive if something happened to me. Richard still believes today David was asking for this to happen to get out on his own. Maybe that was true, because he is much better off today.

Richard and I got engaged in February 1993, and we were planning our wedding for May 1994. In the meantime, my job search was taking time. I took fifteen college-level entry program tests that gave me forty-five credits toward my degree. You have to study on your own and take the tests. I passed these tests for my whole minor in business, and I was very close to my degree. In August 1993, I found a job as a manager in information systems, but the job was fifty-five miles away. I took it and was thrilled to be working again.

Richard and I made it through my unemployed time by the skin of our teeth. I managed money well and had enough to pay one more month of bills when I found a job. That was a lifesaver. It was tough driving fifty-five miles each way every day, but the bills were getting paid, I was engaged to a wonderful man, and I was happy.

Chapter 14

A Wonderful and Crazy Time in My Life

I had a great time planning our wedding for May 1994. I had almost a year to do this, and it was great fun. I invited the whole family from all over the country, and Richard and I found a beautiful golf club to hold the reception. I had my marriage annulled from Dean, so we could get married in the Catholic church. Many people laugh about the annulment. They wonder how you could be with someone for twenty-four years and get your marriage annulled.

The way the church looked at it was that I was very young and had tried getting professional help. Dean was abusive and didn't think he needed any help. I did everything I could to save the marriage. They thought the annulment was appropriate.

Richard and I had to go though the premarital church meetings, and it was kind of weird because most of the people in the class were very young. We attended a couple of times and took various compatibility tests that they give you. The issue of having children of our own was not even a consideration. The last day that they were meeting to discuss children and some of these other issues, we decided not to go back.

Kim had a shower for me and agreed to be my maid of honor. My grandchildren, Gary and Alexandra, were the ring bearer and flower girl. Richard's brother stood up for him, and Tom and David were ushers. My dad walked me down the aisle. It was a beautiful wedding with all my family and friends.

Neither Richard nor I had a real wedding, and both of us had always wanted one. We got the best.

Our first dance was to the song "Unforgettable," and we still dance to it today as a special moment. We spent so much on the wedding that we went to Virginia Beach on our honeymoon and saved some expenses. A great time was had by all.

Things only stay calm for a time when others affect our lives. In August 1994, I graduated from college. Tom graduated from law school, and he agreed to move away with Kim to another state for medical school. They moved in with us for a short time, and Kim was accepted to a medical school in Michigan. Kim moved with the kids to Michigan, and I went out there when she moved to see where they would be staying. She had a little apartment, but it was good for Gary and Alexandra. She had arranged for someone to watch them while she went to school, and Tom stayed with us until he could find a job out there. Tom went out for Thanksgiving, and Kim had a friend of hers whom she went to school with over for dinner. Tom fixed dinner for all of them and then came back to stay with us and continued to look for a job.

He liked his current job but had promised Kim that he would move with her and was trying to follow through on that. Kim was frustrated because he didn't go out to see them enough, but he worked and they had little money. Tom finally got an offer for a job in Michigan and accepted the job. It was close to Christmas, and Tom gave his notice that he would be leaving his current position.

We were getting ready for Christmas and bought the grandkids plenty. I was looking forward to seeing them and having a happy holiday. This would be the first Christmas that Richard and I would spend together as a married couple.

Richard's fiftieth birthday was just before Christmas, so I had a surprise party for him. Kim and the kids were to drive back in time for the party. Tom had given his notice at work, and everything looked like it was working out great—not so.

I got a telephone call from Kim during Richard's party that she and the kids were not on their way home, and to my surprise, she had found a boyfriend. Tom and I talked to her and just asked that she come home with the kids. It was a very emotional time for all of us, and we wanted to make sure they all got home safely. What a way to ruin a party! Tom immediately called his boss and rescinded his resignation.

Kim and the kids came home just before Christmas. Kim wanted a divorce, and that was it. She had a boyfriend, and as far as I was concerned, she acted a bit lovesick over him because they weren't together for the holiday. It was ironic that the guy she was lovesick over was the person Tom cooked Thanksgiving dinner for while he was in Michigan. I had to give Tom credit—he was very mature and handled the situation well. I knew he was upset, but for the sake of his kids, he kept it to himself. I was disappointed that Kim handled it so badly. It appeared to me that Tom wasn't even given a chance after all those years. She was being so foolish.

Kim had been pouting and feeling sorry for herself through all of our Christmas with the kids. We were all downstairs on Christmas Eve trying to make it nice, and she was upstairs on the phone with her boyfriend or alone. I thought this was horrible, because she had two children to think about. I wasn't going to get into a battle with her over the holidays, so we all just made the best of it. Santa came, and she wasn't involved. She was more worried about herself and her friend.

Tom, Kim, and the kids were to go south for her dad's wedding after Christmas. They had already bought the tickets, and they all went for the wedding. I was surprised that Tom would go under those circumstances, but he did. They all left for her dad's, and while she was down there, she arranged to change her flight and go to Ohio to meet her friend for New Year's Eve. She left Tom and the kids with her dad and flew back early. What a bunch of crap! At that time, I was disgusted.

Tom and the kids flew home and stayed with Richard and I until things could get settled. Kim and Tom got divorced.

Alexandra cried herself to sleep many nights because she missed her mom. Tom took care of the kids, made their lunches, did their laundry, was involved in their outside activities, and worked. We shared the cooking for dinner and made the best of it. I didn't want to interfere and knew that Tom had to be both Mom and Dad for a while.

He did a great job with those kids and had a wonderful attitude. He never misspoke about their mother to any of us and tried to save for a place of their own as soon as he could. They were with us for a little over a year, and much of that time was a blur. Kim came home to see the kids a few times. One time she had her boyfriend and wanted me to meet him. I didn't accept everything that was going on, especially with Tom and the kids living with us, so I declined.

She went back to Michigan, eventually broke up with this guy, and met someone else. About the spring of 1996, Tom and the kids moved out and bought a home of their own. I missed them but knew it was for the best. They visited often and spent a lot of time with us. Alexandra was more adjusted to her mom being gone and was very close and protective of her father.

Richard and I were finally all alone and started to remodel the house. We knocked out the wall between our room and Kim's old room and combined them. We made a beautiful bedroom suite and worked on other issues in the house. We were actually preparing to sell at some time.

During the summer of 1995, I planned a cruise for my mom and dad's fiftieth anniversary. I had never been on a cruise, but it was for Mom and Dad. Forty-five relatives and friends went on the cruise. Mom and Dad had a great time, and I am glad we did it. Kim went with her new boyfriend and some friends of theirs. David was not in any position to be able to go and stayed home. I found out that I am not a cruiser, and that will be my last. I sometimes refer to it as my vacation from hell—fly across the country, get on a ship, and fly back home. I don't like flying, and I'm afraid of the deep water. I enjoyed the time spent with the family but would prefer to be on land.

Mom and Dad came out to visit in July 1996. My dad had been diagnosed with lung cancer after returning from the cruise. He was undergoing chemo and appeared to be doing well. We had a big Fourth of July picnic at our home with several family members and friends attending. Aunt Catherine and my cousin Theresa had traveled to our home from Michigan for the picnic.

My mom was thrilled to have her sister with us. My cousin Theresa and I wanted to take our moms to New York for dinner and to see a play. Neither of them had ever gone before. It was a great opportunity for us, and David would be home with my dad during the day. I left responsibility up to my mom for clearing it with dad, and we headed for New York City.

Richard worked during the day and planned to come home and fix something for them to eat. I called to check in while we were at a nice French restaurant having a great time. This was a big mistake. Richard answered the phone and said everything was going fine and for us to have a good time. Next thing I know, my dad was yelling to talk to me. He got on the phone and told me that my husband was a no-good so-and-so. I asked to talk to Richard, and he told me that Dad had been drinking when he got home and was in one of his moods. Some things never change.

That put a damper on our dinner and play, but we went anyway. I knew that when we got home, things would be crazy; they were. Richard was upstairs in our room, and Dad was downstairs yelling and calling him names. My sister Marie and her husband were also at the house.

I went upstairs, and Richard said that while he was cooking dinner, Dad was lying down on the floor downstairs and knew dinner was being prepared. David was being lazy and stayed in his room. Richard prepared dinner and sat down to eat. He thought Dad might me sleeping. My dad came upstairs and threw a fit because he was not called to dinner. This was typical crap when Dad was drunk. He always expected you to tiptoe around him in order to not make him more upset. I couldn't blame Richard for his reaction, because he had not seen Dad like this before.

I honestly believe Dad was ticked off because we left him at home, and Mom didn't bother to ask for his permission to go to New York. I was very upset and disgusted with my dad for getting drunk and being a jerk. I had seen this too much in life and would not make any excuses for him. I didn't talk to him, and Marie took him to her house. She was his savior for the evening and for the next two weeks.

He stayed at Marie's house for the rest of the vacation. Mom stayed with us overnight until Aunt Catherine and Theresa left the next day. She then went to Marie's. I didn't see either one of them for the rest of their stay, and they went home.

I was very upset about the situation with my father, but after all those years at home and putting up with Dean, I decided enabling him was not my job anymore. After a few months, I had telephone conversations with my dad. They were brief but polite with no discussion about what had happened. He once started to discuss it, and I changed the subject. I thought he was wrong, and nothing was going to change my mind.

About a year after they returned to California, my mother told me Dad was not doing too well, and my brothers and sisters had gone out to see him at different times. My cousin Michelle called one day and said that Dad was not well, and I had better go out to see him. I guess denial is all I can say about the subject. At that point in time, I decided not to go out to see my dad.

I was tired of traveling fifty-five miles each way to work and was looking for another position closer to home. I interviewed with a local company and was offered a position close to home. It was a great job, and the offer was too much to turn down. I accepted the position, gave my notice, and decided to go home to see Dad before starting the new job. I don't think that I really believed Dad was seriously ill at that time. I asked Richard to go with me, and although he was hesitant, he finally agreed.

When we got to the house, a couple of my sisters were there. Marie had been there for a few weeks helping take care of Dad. They had a hospital bed in the dining room and hospice came in regularly. Mom said Dad had a couple of inoperable brain tumors; the lung cancer had gone to his brain. Richard and I were tired from the long trip and were staying at a hotel. I went up to my dad and told him that we were going to the hotel and would be back the next day.

He said, "Take care of yourself for the next twenty years."

I said, "Okay, Dad. See you tomorrow." And we left.

From what I understand, they all sat and watched a video of our family that Marie had put together for the fiftieth wedding anniversary party. Dad was commenting about everything and everyone and then went to sleep. The next day when I got there, he didn't recognize anyone or communicate at all. It was such a dramatic change in twelve hours.

Richard and I spent the day with the family and Dad. He wasn't communicating, but I did try to talk to him and tell some jokes. We went to the store and bought steaks for the grill and a Boston crème pie—Dad's favorite. We had a nice dinner, but Mom had to feed Dad. He ate the filet and the pie. These were some of his favorite foods. Richard and I often talk about the fact that the argument at our home was over a meal that he had cooked for Dad. Richard cooked the steaks, and this was Dad's last meal.

We came back the next day to visit and celebrate my niece's birthday. Marie wanted to go to church with Mom and me and leave Richard with Dad. Richard said no. He didn't want to be left alone with Dad, because he was afraid something would happen while we were gone and that he would be blamed. Marie was not happy with this and thought Richard was just being difficult. I could understand his concern, and we did not leave him alone with Dad.

It was so hot in the house; it must have been ninety-eight degrees. The windows were closed, because Dad was cold a lot. My parents did not have air conditioning, so we all dealt with the heat. It was around six o'clock that evening when Jerry's wife, Susie, and I went to check on Dad. He had passed away.

My brother Ted had arranged to have a company come to the house and get Dad after he'd passed away. He had signed a living will, but we were told to wait two hours before calling anyone.

I decided that it was a good time to have a good old Irish tradition and opened a bottle of wine. We all started drinking and talking about old times with Dad. Someone called the church to have the priest come over to the house. By the time he got there, he found us all talking and laughing about times with the family and Dad. I think he thought we were a little strange, because during the conversations, we were laughing and joking. I do believe Dad would have understood this. It took quite a few days for everyone to get home, so we spent the time fixing up some things in the house. Dad was never one to do a lot at home. I don't think it had ever been painted. Richard talked my mom into letting him paint a few of the rooms to spruce it up some.

We had a nice funeral for Dad. My sisters put together collages of pictures for the church, and Mom had a nice-sized picture of Dad in his marine uniform. We brought all these for the service, and they played some of Dad's favorite Irish songs. This was different, especially in a Catholic church.

When we went to the cemetery, there was a military service with the gun salute. Family and friends went back to the house for food and drinks. The Irish always have their drinks. I know my dad did. He would have liked what we put together for him. Richard and I left and headed for home, and I started my new job soon after.

Chapter 15

Life Goes On

In 1997, Richard and I celebrated my fiftieth birthday in the Carolinas. We visited the Wilmington and Raleigh areas and had a great time. I liked my new job managing and relocating a data center. The money was good, and I was much closer to home. I had been using a headhunter to fill positions, and after returning from the Carolinas, I mentioned my interest in relocating to the headhunter.

Richard and I thought it would be great if I could find a position in the Carolinas to relocate us. We would then be in a good area to retire but have a company to move us there before retiring. I told one of the headhunters that if he ever had a request in the southern states to give me a call.

It was the week of Christmas in 1998 when I got a call about a job in the Atlanta area. I agreed to a phone interview over the holiday. The company asked me to come down for an interview in January. I had mentioned at Christmas dinner that I was interviewing for a job in Atlanta. Gary was visibly upset and didn't want us to move. I just told him that I was interviewing and not moving yet. I was scheduled to fly out on a Friday, but we had a snowstorm. I had to reschedule for the following week. I don't think that I really believed at that time that we would be moving anywhere.

The weather finally changed, and the interview went very well. The company wanted me to bring Richard down and check things out to determine whether the position and the area would be a good fit for us. We went down on Valentine's weekend, and Richard liked the area and thought it could be a nice place to live. We went home, and the company made me a great offer. Unfortunately, I had to start the middle of March and had not anticipated moving away in such a short time. I really needed more time to get things squared away but was not being offered more time. I had to make a quick decision, so Richard and I agreed that the time was right for us. The company paid all our expenses for travel, selling our old home, and buying our new home. They gave us additional funds, and I headed to Atlanta to start my new job.

Richard had the responsibility of getting things in order at our house, and I found a small apartment. He had agreed to quit his job and find another when we moved. It was tough living apart. I went home once a month and helped as much as I could. I would visit the kids when home and help out as much as I could. Gary and Alexandra were assured that we would be there for them, and they would visit often. The house sold quickly, and by the first of June, Richard and I were in our new home in Georgia. It was tough leaving the grandkids, and I missed them a lot. That was the biggest adjustment for me.

I loved my new job, and within a year, I was promoted to director of information services. We were able to travel with my new job and went to California to help Mom get rid of things at home and clean the house up. The house was not in good shape and needed a lot of work. She decided to sell and move to Georgia, because it was much cheaper and she could buy a home and pay for it. I had not lived around my mom since I was fifteen years old, and this was different for me. She is very independent and spends a lot of time traveling to visit my brother and sisters.

It is now 2002 and we are doing well and saving for our retirement in the future. We take the grandkids on vacations, and at this time, they are in their teen years. David was having problems and hanging out with the wrong people, so he sold his condo. He was able to make a good sum of money from the sale and has moved in with his dad. Kim is now a doctor and remarried. Tom has a great career, is remarried, and has two other daughters. Gary and Alexandra are living with their father and his new family; they visit their mother often. Everyone has settled down, and things are quite nice and looking good for the future.

Richard and I are together and very happy with our new life together. Could it be the calm before the storm? Things happen that we may not have any direct control over; it is how we handle those things that can be most important. In my life, makin' it right has not been easy. I have made mistakes, and if it were possible, I would change many of the decisions I have made over the years. But that is not what life is all about. We have to make decisions and then live with the outcome.

Each day, we have a choice to make, and that leads us toward a result. It could be positive or negative. People often claim that they don't have choices. Like Bucky told me, you have choices; you just may not like them. He was very right, and I thank him for that bit of advice. In the end, I have learned that for me, the best thing may be to take responsibility, make a decision, and then just let it go.

Chapter 16

My Thoughts

I got involved in adult situations at a very young age. Being pregnant and taking responsibility for a family was very difficult for me. I worked hard to help support my family, take care of my children, and continue my education. My career was very fulfilling, and finally getting a college degree was quite an accomplishment. My future and my retirement are secure; however, as I think back over the years, I wonder what could have been done to make things easier in life.

As a child, it is difficult to understand or comprehend dysfunction in a family. I had my dreams for the future that kept me going. As a good student, I could have immersed myself in school, but my dream of having a husband and children did not include higher education. I remember watching Cinderella and waiting for Prince Charming or seeing Fred Astaire dancing with Ginger Rodgers and thinking what a great couple they made. I think my dreams were fairy tales that kept me pursuing happiness in my life.

I was headed down a path looking for Prince Charming and was determined to find him. Moving away at thirteen may have been a blessing, because the people I hung around with before moving were going nowhere.

Getting involved with someone at such a young age robs you of your youth, and you give a lot up to start an adult life too soon. I can't say that I would have changed anything today about having my children so young other than if I had them later in life, I may have been a better mother. Trying to be a mother to children when you are a child is not easy, and they can suffer from that.

My experiences while pregnant with Kim were harsh, and the unwed mothers' home was good for me. It got me away from my family, and I met a lot of people of all ages in different situations. At the time, however, I thought Prince Charming was going to come and take me away some day, and that made it easier to stay there.

My mother warned me about going out with friends to parties and getting into trouble while Dean was overseas. I thought I could handle it. Emotionally, I was too naïve and unhappy with my situation. I realized that Dean was not that Prince Charming and was hurt by his nonchalant way of looking at being faithful in marriage. That should have been no excuse for me to act the way I did, but as a young girl, I did not always see the forest for the trees.

Dean and I ended up with a dysfunctional family for our children as well. I have often heard that dysfunction follows from family to family unless a real change takes place. I think that real change is a good counselor and lots of self-help.

Tolerating the physical and verbal abuse will always be something I could have changed. I often think walking out with the children and leaving Dean would have been best for all of us. Dean and I have been divorced for years, and my children still can't talk about me in front of him. I do think it is his way of controlling them today—Dad gets upset if they mention Mom. If I use this as a guide, what would he have been like with young children and divorced? Reasonable divorced people have a difficult time dealing with extended families and the children. Dean is definitely not one of those reasonable people.

Now, I understand a little of where women are coming from when they put up with abusive husbands. The alternatives are not always great, and some men will go to any extreme to get back at you. The abusive man doesn't think of the potential consequences as a result of hurting or even killing someone. The only thing I can say is that I was not married to someone who wanted to go to jail as a result of his actions. His concern was not whether he hurt me; it was more about what may happen to him if he went to jail.

In addition, Dean is the type of person who wants others to think well of him. He hit me in places that were easy to hide from others. To others, he was such a nice guy. This is an example of how much we may really know about a person by just looking at what they want us to see.

Many women have dealt with severe abuse and been beat up badly, so it is obvious to anyone that they have been hurt. If the police are called, some of these men actually go to jail today. Many women don't press charges and go back on the roller coaster for another time. I understand the thought process that battered women go through, wondering if maybe they caused the argument that led to the man losing his temper. After all, the abuser tells the woman that she is the problem and deserves to be punished.

I, along with other women, accept the outcome and responsibility for the man losing his temper. Crazy as it seems, we use these excuses to avoid doing anything about it until we have had enough and seek help. I found many reasons not to leave; until I was ready, I stayed with Dean. I was afraid of my father and ended up being afraid of my husband. Until I sought help, had counseling, and stopped fearing him, I was stuck. Finally, leaving was the best thing I did for myself and my children.

It is very difficult when you are in the middle of the weeds to find your way out. In the end, I do know that I needed a lot of counseling and found it. I often wonder what would have happened if I had gotten counseling sooner in life. I ended up throwing myself into my children, education, and a career and that was my lifesaver.

I will always believe that I tried everything to make my marriage work until the day I left. Breaking up a family cannot be taken lightly, and we have all seen the impact it has on others, especially the children. Extended families are often difficult to adjust to, because they may have spouses or ex-spouses who have agendas that impact everyone. Some people can be very self-serving and end up hurting their children without even realizing it.

Dysfunction follows families through generations. Divorce does the same. Some say that if we get married young, we don't understand the impact on everyone involved and our youth is the problem. Getting married young is not always the issue as far as I am concerned. People often do as they wish and do not consider others when it comes to relationships. They use the excuse that age is the gauge and think they are smarter or more mature because they are older.

As mature adults, we may eventually understand that none of us are perfect, and we do have an impact on others, especially our children. Some adults don't ever reach this place in life. They stay stuck, and so do their children and generations to come—until the cycle is broken.